Magellan's Unlikely Explorers

*A collage of experiences through
a wide swatch of history.*

Magellan's
Unlikely Explorers

Stories of the
First Circumnavigation

John Sailors

ISBN-13: 978-1-938688-19-5

This book is set in Garamond, with block quotes in Centaur.
The author's name on the cover is set in Optima, an elegant
sans serif typeface with thick-thin contrast,
like the author. (Some people
think too much.)

Find some history:
EnriqueOfMalacca.com
Twitter: @CircumNavgating
Facebook.com/Circumnavigating

May we all find our own Spice Island.

For Jessie,
for encouragement and patience.

Contents

1. Magellan's Unlikely Crew   11

2. Antonio Pigafetta: Scholar, Explorer, Anthropologist, and More   14

3. Charles V, Magellan, and Columbus   23

4. Mapping the World   29

5. Francisco Albo and His Navigational Log   37

6. Cartagena and Mutiny at Puerto San Julián   41

7. Paulo and the Patagonian Giants   45

8. Juan Serrano and the Santiago Shipwreck   51

9. Joãozito Lopes Carvalho: First Brazilian Native to Cross the Pacific   54

10. Duarte Barbosa and Portuguese India   65

11. Ferdinand Magellan's Real Circumnavigation   73

12. Gómez de Espinosa: Master-at-Arms   77

13. Magellan and the Battle of Mactan   79

14. Espinosa: Unlikely Captain-General   84

15. Juan Sebastián Elcano Circles the Globe   87

16. Jules Verne, Pigafetta, and That Pesky International Date Line   89

17. The Circumnavigation of Sir John Mandeville   93

18. A World Already Mapped   95

19. Enrique of Malacca: First Circumnavigator   98

Having heard that a fleet composed of five vessels had been fitted out in the city of Seville for the purpose of going to discover the Spice Islands of Maluco, under command of Captain-general Fernando de Magaglianes ... I set out from the city of Barcelona ... bearing many letters in my favor ...

—Antonio Pigafetta, unlikely explorer, anthropologist, and palm wine enthusiast.

1.

Magellan's Unlikely Crew

NOTHING ABOUT FERDINAND MAGELLAN'S EXPEDITION was textbook. Magellan planned to sail to the farthest point yet reached in the East, but get there sailing westward and south off the map. There he would locate and sail through a magical strait that would deliver his fleet to Balboa's South Sea, where Magellan could swoop into Asia and open a new trade route to the fabled Spice Islands. It was something Columbus and others had failed to do.

Making the expedition more unlikely, Magellan was a Portuguese *fidalgo* (noble) sailing for rival Spain—itself the newly united Castile and Aragon—whose new king was an eighteen-year-old Habsburg from Flanders who would one day, briefly, be sovereign over record real estate around the globe.

From the start and along the way Magellan fought intrigue, sabotage, and mutiny and from several directions, that while struggling to keep a crew of several hundred men, crammed into five ships, afloat, operating, and moving.

He was also forced to take some seasonal rolls of the dice in terms of weather: Magellan would not have named the South Sea "Pacifico" (calm) if he happened to cross it during typhoon season, and we probably wouldn't know his name at all today if he had.

Somehow through so much, small bits of his crew hung on and ultimately completed an unplanned circumnavigation of the globe.

The Crew

On September 20, 1519, Magellan's Armada de Molucca departed Sanlúcar de Barrameda, south of Seville, with five ships and around 260 men, two-thirds of them Spanish, the rest Portuguese (31), Italian (29), and French (17), as well as Flemish, Greek, German, Austrian, Irish, English, and other.[1] Among them was a young Malay slave named Enrique who became the first person to circle the globe to where his own language was spoken, and possibly the first human to circumnavigate the earth.

Others were picked up along the way, including pilots, a few hostages in Brunei, and kidnapped Patagonian giants. In Brazil, a seven-year-old joined the expedition as a cabin boy and became the first native of that region to cross the Pacific Ocean.

Spanish and Portuguese expeditions of the day struggled to find crews. Ships needed professional mariners to keep afloat, often men raised in port cities who took to sea as a livelihood. But the supply of such men was limited, in Seville more so than in Lisbon. Fleets were forced to sign men who had no experience at sea but were seeking to escape, many fleeing arrest, jail, or debtors' prison, or abandoning families and dreary lives on land.

Pages and cabin boys as young as eight filled some of the gaps in the roster.

For Magellan the outlook was even bleaker. Spanish officials insisted on a primarily Spanish crew, but few Spanish seamen were willing to serve a Portuguese commander. Prospective hires also cited low wages—in Castile there were opportunities on land that didn't have the mortal dangers involved in going to sea.

Magellan tried to sign several Portuguese crew members that Spanish officials denied, though a few hid their origins so they could join the fleet. In the end Magellan sailed with a fleet that was fairly international.

Of course, it took more than sailors to keep ships afloat. Magellan's armada carried caulkers, coopers, carpenters, and blacksmiths; stewards, barbers (medieval doctors), and chaplains; not to mention gunners, cross-bowmen, and men-at-arms.

From the Trinidad Roster

Ferdinand Magellan	Captain general	Portugal	Died, Mactan, 4/27/1521
Estêvão Gomes	Pilot major	Portugal	Deserted
Giovanni Battista di Polcevera	Master	Genoa	Died, Mozambique, 1526
Francisco Albo	Master's mate	Rhodes	Returned to Spain, 1522
Gonzalo Gómez de Espinosa	Master-at-arms	Castile	Returned to Spain, 1527

Also aboard Trinidad

Duarte Barbosa	Supernumerary[2]	Portugal	Died, Cebu, 5/01/1521
Enrique of Malacca	Interpreter	Malacca	Last seen on Cebu, 1521
Antonio Pigafetta	Supernumerary	Lombardy	Returned to Spain, 1522
Cristovão Rebêlo[3]	Supernumerary	Portugal	Died, Mactan, 4/27/1521

The nationalities of men in some of these key roles stood to make or break the expedition. Distrustful Spanish officials appointed the captain of the fleet's largest ship, a prominent Castilian, as inspector-general of the fleet—a check on Magellan's authority. Two other ships' captains were also Castilian and hostile to their Portuguese captain-general.

And just as the armada set out, Magellan received a secret communique from Diogo Barbosa, his father-in-law, warning of a conspiracy by the Castilian captains to mutiny and even kill Magellan to take control of the fleet.

This was the implausible crew that began the first circumnavigation.

---

1. It's uncertain how many men sailed with the expedition. Records and rosters were incomplete and not always reliable. Historians usually put the number between 240 and 270.

2. *Supernumeraries* (sohresalientes) were extras brought on voyages.

3. Some historians believe Cristovão Rabêlo was Magellan's illegitimate son. Magellan listed him in his will in 1519. At Cebu after Magellan removed Duarte Barbosa as captain of the *Victoria*, Rabêlo was named to replace him. The young man was killed days later along with Magellan in the Battle of Mactan, April 27, 1521. The Spanish spelling is Cristóbal Ravelo.

2.

Antonio Pigafetta: Scholar, Explorer, Anthropologist, and More

On Monday morning August 10, St. Lawrence's day in the year abovesaid, the fleet, having been supplied with all the things necessary for the sea, (and counting those of every nationality, we were two hundred and thirty-seven men), made ready to leave the harbor of Seville. Discharging many pieces of artillery, the ships held their foresails to the wind and descended the river Betis ...

ANTONIO PIGAFETTA WAS NOT a sailor or mariner, not a navigator or explorer, but a papal ambassador's aide traveling to Spain when he just happened to hear about a five-ship fleet preparing to sail across the "South Sea," one of the few stretches of the globe Europeans had yet to chart.

Pigafetta not only rushed to sign on; he became historically the most important member of Ferdinand Magellan's roughly 260-man crew.

Among the roles he took on during the three-year journey were explorer, chronicler, anthropologist, linguist, and palm wine enthusiast, and importantly, he lived to tell his tale: Pigafetta was among the eighteen worn and starving survivors on the *Victoria* when it returned to Seville in September 1522.

Pigafetta's Unlikely Travel Journal

Pigafetta kept a daily journal that he later compiled into the manuscript(s) we know today. The original was lost, but four copies survived, three in French and one in Italian. (The excerpts in this book are English translations from the Italian manuscript.)

Pigafetta's richly detailed account stands out among travelogues and chronicles kept on other expeditions. He managed to gather substantial detail about the cultures, lifestyles, and languages of the peoples they came across—often amazingly fast—including the Tupi

Pigafetta.[1]

people in Brazil, the Patagonian "giants" in South America, the Chamorros in Guam, and peoples in the modern-day Philippines. He also gives rich accounts of Brunei and the Moluccas.

Pigafetta's journal gives us the bulk of what we know about the Magellan-Elcano expedition; it tells of the wonders of the first journey through the strait, the horrors of the first Pacific crossing, and the unplanned final leg of the voyage that resulted in the first circumnavigation. It recorded the human side of the journey, as well, chronicling the spirit and emotions of the sometimes-jubilant, sometimes-terrified crew, and the adventures of Pigafetta himself.

Magellan's goal was to find a new route to Asia, and that meant sailing well into the unknown, far off the map, with the crew facing all the fears entailed. Among their concerns was the very reason the map ended where it did, at the farthest point charted. Pigafetta explained:

> That place is called the cape of Santa Maria, and it was formerly thought that one passed thence to the sea of Sur [the Pacific] ... but nothing further was ever discovered. ... A Spanish captain called Johan de Solis and sixty men, who were going to discover lands like us, were formerly eaten at that river by those cannibals because of too great confidence.

To the crew this was a journey to places where few humans had ventured before, where legends warned of bizarre creatures—three-hundred-foot-long eels and man-size lobsters, not to mention wild beasts with wings.

Soon after crossing the Atlantic, they encountered their first exotic creature, for most of them a never-before-seen bird.

> Truly, the great number of those geese cannot be reckoned; in one hour we loaded the five ships. Those geese are black and have all their feathers alike both on body and wings. They do not fly, and live on fish. They were so fat that it was not necessary to pluck them but to skin them. Their beak is like that of a crow.

Five hundred years later, readers might be surprised to learn how easy it is to skin one of the planet's most beloved birds, the penguin.

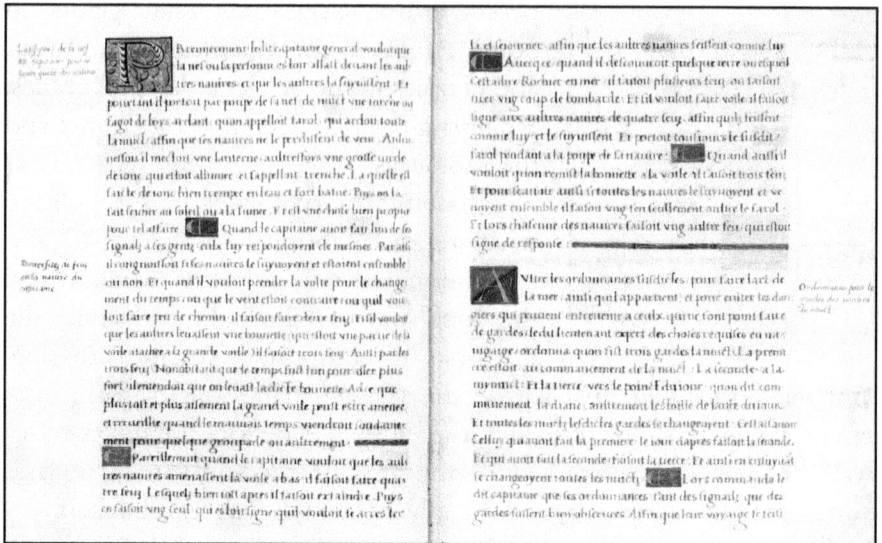

Opening pages of a Pigafetta manuscript.

And penguins weren't the only freakish birds they found.

> I saw many kinds of birds, among them one that had no anus; and
> another, when the female wishes to lay its eggs, it does so on the back
> of the male and there they are hatched. The latter bird has no feet, and
> always lives in the sea.

> [There is] another kind which live on the ordure [excrement] of the
> other birds, and in no other manner; for I often saw this bird, which is
> called Cagassela, fly behind the other birds, until they are constrained to
> drop their ordure, which the former seizes immediately and abandons
> the latter bird.

And true to legend, many exotic creatures were found in the sea
itself.

> I also saw many flying fish, and many others collected together, so that
> they resembled an island.

> In that Ocean Sea one sees a very amusing fish hunt. The fish [that
> hunt] are of three sorts ... Those fish follow the flying fish, which are
> one palmo and more in length and very good to eat. When the above
> three kinds [of fish] find any of those flying fish, the latter immediately
> leap from the water and fly as long as their wings are wet—more than

a crossbow's flight. While they are flying, the others run along back of them under the water following the shadow of the flying fish. The latter have no sooner fallen into the water than the others immediately seize and eat them.

It is a very amusing thing to watch.

… Those sea-wolves are of various colors and as large as a calf, with a head like that of a calf, ears small and round, and large teeth. They have no legs but only feet with small nails attached to the body, which resemble our hands, and between their fingers the same kind of skin as the geese. They would be very fierce if they could run.

Novel foods were to be found as well. In Brazil, the variety was remarkable.

There we got a plentiful refreshment of fowls, potatoes, many sweet pine-apples—in truth the most delicious fruit that can be found—the flesh of the anta [a hoofed animal], which resembles beef, sugarcane, and innumerable other things, which I shall not mention in order not to be prolix.

We see Pigafetta most fully when he describes the coconut, a food that appealed to the anthropologist in him, as well as the palm wine enthusiast.

Cocoanuts are the fruit of the palmtree. Just as we have bread, wine, oil, and milk, so those people get everything from that tree.

They get wine in the following manner. They bore a hole into the heart of the said palm at the top called palmito [i.e., stalk], from which distils a liquor which resembles white must. That liquor is sweet but somewhat tart, and [is gathered] in canes [of bamboo] as thick as the leg and thicker. They fasten the bamboo to the tree at evening for the morning, and in the morning for the evening.

That palm bears a fruit, namely, the cocoanut, which is as large as the head or thereabouts. Its outside husk is green and thicker than two fingers. Certain filaments are found in that husk, whence is made cord for binding together their boats. Under that husk there is a hard shell, much thicker than the shell of the walnut, which they burn and make therefrom a powder that is useful to them.

Under that shell there is a white marrowy substance one finger in thickness, which they eat fresh with meat and fish as we do bread; and it has a taste resembling the almond. It could be dried and made into bread.

When the natives wish to make oil, they take that cocoanut, and allow the marrowy substance and the water to putrefy. Then they boil it and it becomes oil like butter. When they wish to make vinegar, they allow only the water to putrefy, and then place it in the sun, and a vinegar results like [that made from] white wine. ...

A family of ten persons can be supported on two trees, by utilizing them [weekly] about for the wine; for if they did otherwise, the trees would dry up. They last a century."

Somehow Pigafetta was able to learn all this from the Visayans they first met in the Philippines, in a short time and with no knowledge of their language.

Pigafetta's Vocabulary Samples

Pigafetta found a method of recording sample vocabularies of languages they encountered, from that of the Tupi people in Brazil to the Chamorros on Guam. His ability to collect word lists in often a very short time baffles historians today.

Pigafetta's language samples give us the first record of several languages and a window into the minds of sixteenth-century Europeans in the vocabulary Pigafetta chose. Among them were the names of foods, animals, parts of the body including genitalia, and gods and demons.

Writing about the Patagonians, likely the Tehuelches, Pigafetta explained his method:

That giant whom we had in our ship told me those words; for when he, upon asking me for capac, that is to say, bread, as they call that root which they use as bread, and oli, that is to say, water, saw me write those words quickly, and afterward when I, with pen in hand, asked him for other words, he understood me. All [these] words are pronounced in the throat, for such is their method of pronunciation.

Vocabulary of the Patagonians.

Despite this explanation, scholars are perplexed at Pigafetta's ability to compile these lexicons so quickly.

Sample of the words with English:

head	her	armpit	salischin	gem	sechegi
eye	other	breast	ochii	dog	holl
nose	or	thumb	ochon	wolf	ani
eyebrows	occhechel	body	gechel	dead bird	hoihoi
eyelids	sechechiel	penis	scachet	ship	theu
nostrils	oresche	testicles	sacaneos	water	oli
mouth	xiam	vagina	isse	fire	ghialeme
lips	schiahame	intercourse	iohoi	smoke	giaiche
teeth	phor	thigh	chiaue	no	ehen
tongue	schial	knee	tepin	sun	calexcheni
chin	sechen	rump	schiachen	stars	settere
hair	aschir	heart	thol	sea	aro
face	cogechel	old man	calischen	wind	oni
throat	ohumer	young man	callemi	big devil	Setebos
shoulders	peles	gold	pelpeli	small devil	Cheleule

Pigafetta and Magellan

Wrote Pigafetta of the battle of Mactan:

> So many of them charged down upon us that they shot the captain
> through the right leg with a poisoned arrow. On that account, he ordered
> us to retire slowly, but the men took to flight, except six or eight of us
> who remained with the captain. ... Recognizing the captain, so many
> turned upon him that they knocked his helmet off his head twice, but
> he always stood firmly like a good knight, together with some others. ...

At least by his own dramatic account, Pigafetta was one of six or
eight men who stood their ground beside Magellan in the battle at
Mactan, where Magellan was killed. Pigafetta himself was wounded—
an injury that may have saved his life; it kept him from attending the
banquet at Cebu four days later, which turned out to be an ambush.

Throughout his journal, Pigafetta heaps praise on Magellan. He
became a loyal confidant, sailing aboard the flagship *Trinidad* along
with others close to the Captain-General: Duarte Barbosa, Magellan's
brother-in-law; Cristovão Rabêlo, another relation and possibly
Magellan's illegitimate son; and Enrique of Malacca, Magellan's slave-
interpreter.

As for Magellan, he likely appreciated the importance of chroniclers
on expeditions, given his seven years' experience with the Portuguese
in Asia. When Vasco da Gama reached India in 1498, the Portuguese
knew nothing about the region—its geography, its peoples and cultures,
or the area's political and economic rivalries. In fact, da Gama's fleet
believed the Hindus they met in India were eastern Christians, just
with odd ways of worshiping.

Most dangerously, they failed to understand the role the monsoon
winds played along trade routes and spent three deadly months
returning across the Indian Ocean off-season.

Only five years later, the Portuguese had mastered the winds, they
understood the religions, and the viceroys Francisco de Almeida and
Afonso de Albuquerque were able to exploit regional rivalries to
establish a trade empire. This was possible because of hard work put
in by chroniclers who ensured future expeditions would travel with
knowledge gleaned by previous ones.

Pigafetta After the First Circumnavigation

> From the time we left that bay [of San Lucar] until the present day [of our return], we had sailed fourteen thousand four hundred and sixty leguas, and furthermore had completed the circumnavigation of the world from east to west. On Monday, September eight, we cast anchor near the quay of Seville, and discharged all our artillery.

When the *Victoria* returned to Spain in 1522, Charles V invited its final captain, Juan Sebastián Elcano, to report on the journey, bringing with him the two crewmen most knowledgeable about the expedition. On this, Elcano snubbed Pigafetta, evidence the two men did not get along.

But Pigafetta had a story to tell. He had nearly met death several times—at the battle of Mactan, at the massacre on Cebu, and once when he slipped into the ocean and nearly drowned. He had dined with natives and kings in unknown lands, had witnessed incredible feats, had endured the worst of storms, and sailed a full circle around the earth.

First-ever map of the Magellan Strait, drawn by Pigafetta.

Snubbed by Elcano, Pigafetta called on Charles himself to present his account.

Unsatisfied with the reception, Pigafetta traveled next to Portugal to tell his story to King João III and then to France where he met with the queen mother Marie Louise of Savoy. And while Pigafetta was preparing his journal for publication, he was invited to Rome to report on the expedition to Pope Clement VII, and he wound up working at the Vatican briefly.

It was partially due to Pigafetta's efforts that the world came to credit Magellan as the driving force behind the first circumnavigation. Magellan overcame tremendous obstacles including sabotage and fears of assassination just to get the Armada de Molucca launched, and in the worst of circumstances after—storms, shipwrecks, attacks—refused to give up. Pigafetta offered detailed, if sometimes exaggerated, accounts of Magellan's determination and leadership.

Pigafetta's colorful career didn't end with Magellan. The scholar later gave up his day job in Rome to join the Order of Rhodes, a military-religious order, as a knight. Though he fades from history about that time, it is generally believed that Antonio Pigafetta died as a knight fighting the Ottoman Turks.

The beginning of Pigafetta's journal:

> Inasmuch as, most illustrious and excellent Lord, there are many curious persons who not only take pleasure in knowing and hearing the great and wonderful things which God has permitted me to see and suffer during my long and dangerous voyage ...

And the ending:

> Leaving Seviglia, I went to Valladolid, where I presented to his sacred Majesty, Don Carlo, neither gold nor silver, but things very highly esteemed by such a sovereign. Among other things I gave him a book, written by my hand, concerning all the matters that had occurred from day to day during our voyage. I left there as best I could and went to Portagalo where I spoke with King Johanni of what I had seen. Passing through Spagnia, I went to Fransa where I made a gift of certain things from the other hemisphere to the mother of the most Christian king, Don Francisco, Madame the regent. Then I came to Italia, where I established my permanent abode, and devoted my poor labors to the famous and most illustrious lord, Philipo de Villers Lisleadam, the most worthy grand master of Rhodi.

1. Image of Pigafetta: This portrait was traditionally believed to be Antonio Pigafetta, though it may be another Pigafetta, Gio. Alberto of Gerolamo.

3.

Charles V, Magellan, and Columbus

Holy Roman Emperor Charles V.

ERDINAND MAGELLAN'S ROYAL BACKING came as a long shot among long shots. No Castilian monarch would have sponsored a Portuguese captain on so large an expedition, especially a prospect already disloyal to his own country. But Spain suddenly had a foreign king, an eighteen-year-old Habsburg from Flanders with ambitions—and dominions—well beyond Spain.

This was King Carlos I (Holy Roman Emperor Charles V), whose route to the Spanish throne was itself a long shot. Charles was the grandson of Aragon's King Ferdinand and Castile's Queen Isabella, the royal couple whose marriage united Spain. As was the practice in European courts, they looked for further expansion of territory and power through the marriage of their children. For their daughter Joanna of Castile, they arranged a marriage to Philip the Handsome, archduke of Austria. Joanna and Philip were Charles's parents.

Upon Queen Isabella's death, a succession battle ensued that included the poisoning of Philip. His death led to the complete mental breakdown of the already-unstable Joanna—known in history as Juana la Loca (Joanna the Mad). After Philip's death, she kept her husband's embalmed corpse in her bed chamber and even brought it with her when she traveled around the kingdom.

Joanna wound up in protective custody, and after further political battles, Charles finally ascended the throne in March 1516 after Ferdinand's death. The following year he arrived in Valladolid with a huge entourage of Flemish courtiers and German mercenaries. A new Spain had a new king.

Like Christopher Columbus, Magellan sailed for "the Spanish crown," though it was nowhere near that simple for either.

Columbus first approached the Portuguese court with his scheme to sail westward to Asia. Columbus was turned down twice by Portugal and twice by Spanish officials, and he was headed to France to shop his plan there when Ferdinand and Isabella had a change of heart on the enterprise.

As for Magellan, he defected to Spain after a falling-out with his own monarch, Portugal's King Manuel I. Magellan had served Portugal in East Africa and Asia and used his seven years' experience there to promote his plan for a westward expedition. He provided Charles with maps, globes, documents, and people—Enrique of Malacca, a slave Magellan took following the sack of that city, and possibly also a young women from Malacca or Java. At presentations in Valladolid, Enrique, a Malay teenager talented with languages, likely spoke better Spanish than Charles did at the time.

For Castilian officials, a united Spain was already a big deal and wealth was coming in from Columbus's discoveries. But Charles had bigger ambitions. As heir to the reigning Holy Roman emperor, Charles dreamed of going beyond his namesake Charlemagne in creating a world empire. Spain's overseas territory made that possible, but Portugal was winning the race in East Asia and shipping home huge wealth with its annual spice fleets to India.

Thirty years earlier, with the world suddenly theirs for the "discovering," Portugal and Spain sat down and divided the globe in half between them, signing the Treaty of Tordesillas in 1494, which drew a simple line pole to pole.[1] The treaty granted Spain everything to the west and Portugal everything to the east—a useful agreement

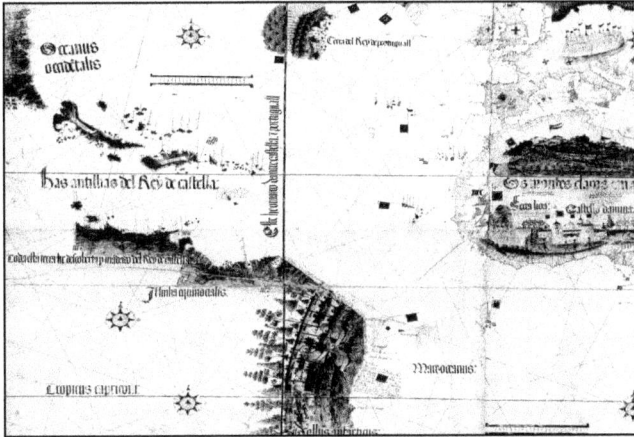

Demarcation line set in the Treaty of Tordesillas, shown on the Cantino map.

for the two Iberian kingdoms, though certainly disturbing to the 50 million people living in established communities in the Americas.

A selling point for a Spanish expedition to the Spice Islands[2] was uncertainty about which side of the demarcation line they lay. Magellan asserted the Moluccas, China, and Japan all lay on the Spanish side.

It has to be noted and restated, "discovering" wasn't about just locating, studying, and adding places to the map; *discovering* meant locating and conquering. In East Africa and India the Portuguese had done just that, building forts in peacefully cooperating cities such as Cochin (Kochi) and invading cities that resisted, from Kilwa in East Africa, to Calicut in India, and Malacca to the south.

Magellan and Columbus certainly had ambitions beyond just exploring. In Magellan's case, he asked for a lot. Among the conditions he requested: ten years of exclusive trade over the route for Magellan and his partner, Rui Faleiro; a twentieth of the profits obtained; the governorship of territories for the partners and their heirs; the right to ship 1,000 ducats worth of merchandise annually with the fleets to the new colonies; and (and here was a big one that Charles did not agree to) overlordship of two islands for themselves and their heirs if they "discovered" more than six.

Charles accepted many of Magellan's conditions, though. Charles, too, was on the move. Between the time he agreed to back Magellan's expedition and its departure, Charles was elected Holy Roman emperor, succeeding his grandfather Maximilian. He became known in history as Holy Roman Emperor Charles V.

Charles's dominions by the time of his death rank among the most extensive in history. The Habsburg monarch became Holy Roman emperor (modern-day Germany), archduke of Austria (and empire), king of Spain (Castile and Aragon), "lord" of the Netherlands, duke of Burgundy, and sovereign of Naples, Sicily, and Sardinia. Charles also became sovereign over the new Spanish colonies in the Americas and Asia—the first empire over which the sun never set.

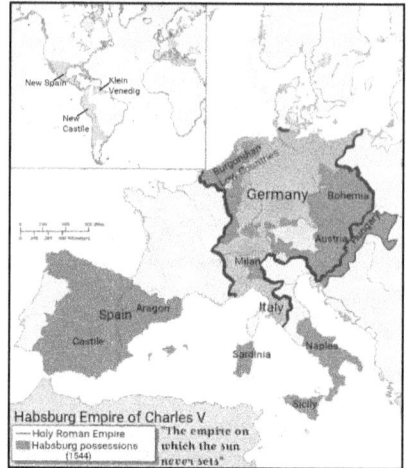

Habsburg Empire of Charles V

His extensive dominions put Charles at the center of major historical events. Charles reigned over the conquest of the Inca and Aztec empires by the Spanish conquistadors. And in Europe he sided with Pope Leo X in 1521 in outlawing Martin Luther—whose reformation kicked off roughly 150 years of war on the continent.

France, which found itself surrounded by Habsburg territory, was a constant enemy. Charles's first war with France began in 1521, not long after Magellan's death in the Philippines and a year before the *Victoria* completed its circumnavigation.

Charles continuously fought the Ottoman Turks, as well, as they expanded their empire up into Hungary.

As for marriage, Charles got to make his own plans, but power and empire building were still the main factors. An alliance with England was originally the focus; Charles was first engaged to an eleven-year-old sister of the future King Henry VIII, Mary. In the end, though, relations with Portugal received priority, and a marriage was arranged with Isabella of Portugal, daughter of King Manual I, whom Magellan had quarreled with.

It was an arranged marriage for political purposes, but it was said that on their first meeting in Seville in 1526, the couple fell deeply in love. Isabella went on to act as regent in Spain during Charles's long absences. The monarch kept no fixed capital and spent much of

Charles and Isabella.

his reign on the road, making some forty journeys from country to country.

In 1556, Charles's dominions were divided between a Spanish Habsburg line and the German-Austrian Habsburgs. The two dynasties remained allies until the Spanish line died out in 1700 with the death of Spain's King Charles II—setting off the thirteen-year War of Spanish Succession that drew in Spain, Austria, France, Great Britain, Savoy, and the Dutch Republic.

---

1. The Treaty of Tordesillas reset the location of a line of demarcation previously established in papal bulls by Pope Alexander VI.

2. The "Spice Islands," or the Moluccas, are a group of islands in eastern Indonesia today known by the local spelling, Malukus. For people new to the area's history, further confusion is added by the name Malacca, the city and sultanate on the Malay Peninsula—which in Malay is spelled Melaka.

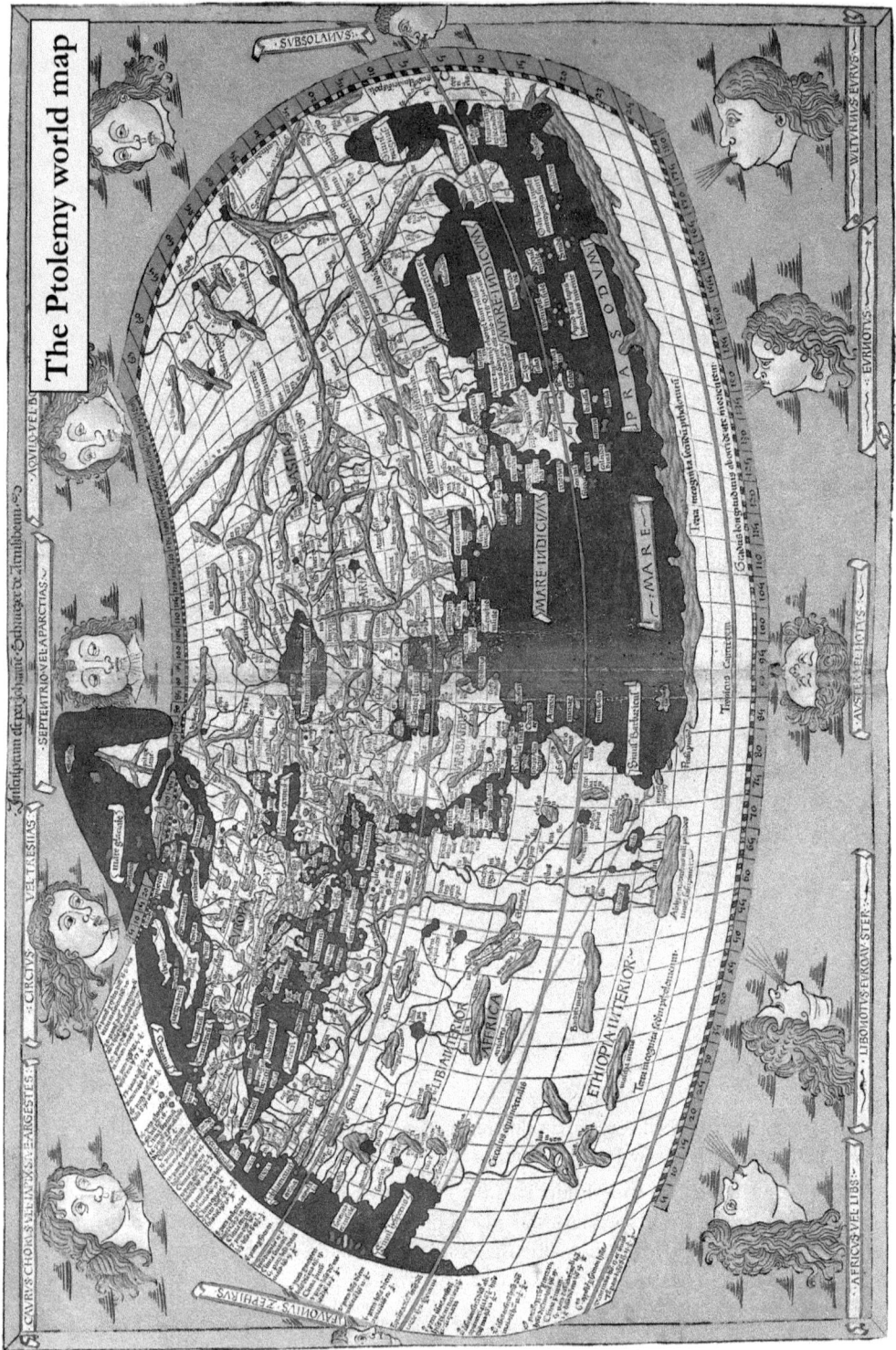

The Ptolemy world map

4.

Mapping the World

IT WASN'T COLUMBUS OR MAGELLAN who proved the world was round. The flat earth notion we hear about today was a medieval phenomenon; by 500 BCE the Greeks had established that the planet was a sphere, and in time estimated its size with surprising accuracy.

In the third century BCE the Greek mathematician Eratosthenes found a simple way of estimating the world's circumference, measuring the noontime altitude of the sun at two locations. He calculated that the earth was about 40,000 kilometers (24,800 miles) in circumference; today that measurement is put at 40,096 kilometers (24,901 miles). Eratosthenes was that close.

While the ancient Greeks mastered the geometry needed to measure the earth, they didn't travel or trade far enough to master its geography. Still, their understanding of the globe provided considerable detail for Renaissance geographers and explorers to start with.

Ptolemy world map

The Ptolemy world map[1] shows the world as it was known in the Greco-Roman world in the second century CE. These maps were created based on descriptions in Claudius Ptolemy's book *Geography*, written about 150 CE. No original maps from the book itself have ever been discovered.

The 1482 version of the Ptolemy world map on the left gives us a picture of what Columbus and Magellan started with. Ptolemy world maps span from Europe to Asia, with the Indian Ocean landlocked to the south. Missing of course are the Pacific Ocean and the Americas. West of Europe is the ever-mysterious ocean sea that Columbus would cross.

Renaissance geographers began to improve on Ptolemy's world view, adding detail from medieval travelers such as Marco Polo and Niccolò de' Conti, and then Portuguese discoveries.

The Fra Mauro map

The Fra Mauro world map

The giant Fra Mauro map at St. George's Castle in Lisbon was the first in Europe to show Africa as a free-standing continent surrounded by a waterway at the far tip.[2] Produced in 1450, it challenged the widely accepted view from Ptolemy that the Indian Ocean was a closed-in sea. It also gave the Portuguese more reason to turn down Columbus's proposal for a westward expedition.

Portugal was a small kingdom on the edge of European civilization. Its isolated geography suddenly offered prospects in Africa. First and immediate were gold and slaves—thus began the Portuguese slave trade in West Africa. Beyond that were dreams of a river route to the Nile and the legendary kingdom of Prester John, and possibly a greater holy grail, a sea route to the Indies bypassing the Middle East and Islam.

The Fra Mauro map is 2.4 X 2.4 meters and oriented to the south (upside down) in the Arab tradition. With gold leaf and minute illustration, the map shows a clear sea route around Africa, with pictures of caravels making the journey. It offers substantial details of the Spice Islands and ports along the Indian Ocean.

In 1488, when Columbus was in Lisbon trying to sell the Portuguese monarch on his plan, Bartolomeu Dias had just returned from the first successful rounding of the Cape of Good Hope. Columbus apparently was present as Dias reported on the journey that had just given Portugal an eastward sea route to India and Asia beyond.

As it worked out, though, Renaissance geographers were under-estimating the earth's size. It's been said that if Columbus and Magellan had Eratosthenes's measurements, they may well have just stayed home.

Columbus

Columbus was one of several people discussing a possible westward route to the Spice Islands as rivals Spain and Portugal raced to claim the fabled sources of cloves, nutmeg, and mace. He calculated Japan was just 4,440 kilometers (2,760 miles) from the Canary Islands, a distance that is actually 19,300 kilometers (12,000 miles).

Until his death Columbus insisted he had reached islands on the eastern edge of Asia. Yet additional landings by Columbus and others began to outline something that appeared more like a continent

Waldseemüller's map

than islands, and it was another navigator pushing this notion who accidentally lent his name to Columbus's discovery.

Martin Waldseemüller's world map

In 1507 the German cartographer Martin Waldseemüller created the first world map (left) to show the Americas as a continent, and needing to identify the landmass, he added the name of an explorer and writer who argued that it was in fact a continent: Amerigo Vespucci. An Italian from Venice, Vespucci had sailed on at least two voyages, one for Spain in 1499–50 and one for Portugal in 1501–02, the latter of which brought him to Brazil.

On Columbus's fourth and final journey to the Americas in 1502–04, five years before Waldseemüller gave them the name, Columbus landed on the Isthmus of Panama after surviving a storm he described as the worst he had ever known. He anchored his fleet briefly to recover and observe Christmas before sailing back to Spain the final time. Had Columbus instead journeyed inland to explore, he would have been surprised to find a very unexpected ocean.

Balboa

Vasco Núñez de Balboa did just that nine years later, in 1513. Using native guides, Balboa led an expedition across the isthmus, where they became the first Europeans to reach the ocean he called Mar del Sur (South Sea). (Presumably the native guides knew the sea was there and may have raised an eyebrow at the Europeans' excitement.)

Himself an unlikely explorer, Balboa first settled on Hispaniola in 1505 as a planter and pig farmer, a profession he failed at. In debt, he escaped by stowing away on a ship bound for modern-day Columbia. Legend says he hid in a barrel along with his dog before being caught.

Later, as a reward for his discoveries, Balboa was named governor of the provinces of Panama and Coiba, but power in the region was held under a new governor of Darién, Pedro Arias Dávila (usually called Pedrarias). In 1519, Pedrarias was struggling to hold onto power and,

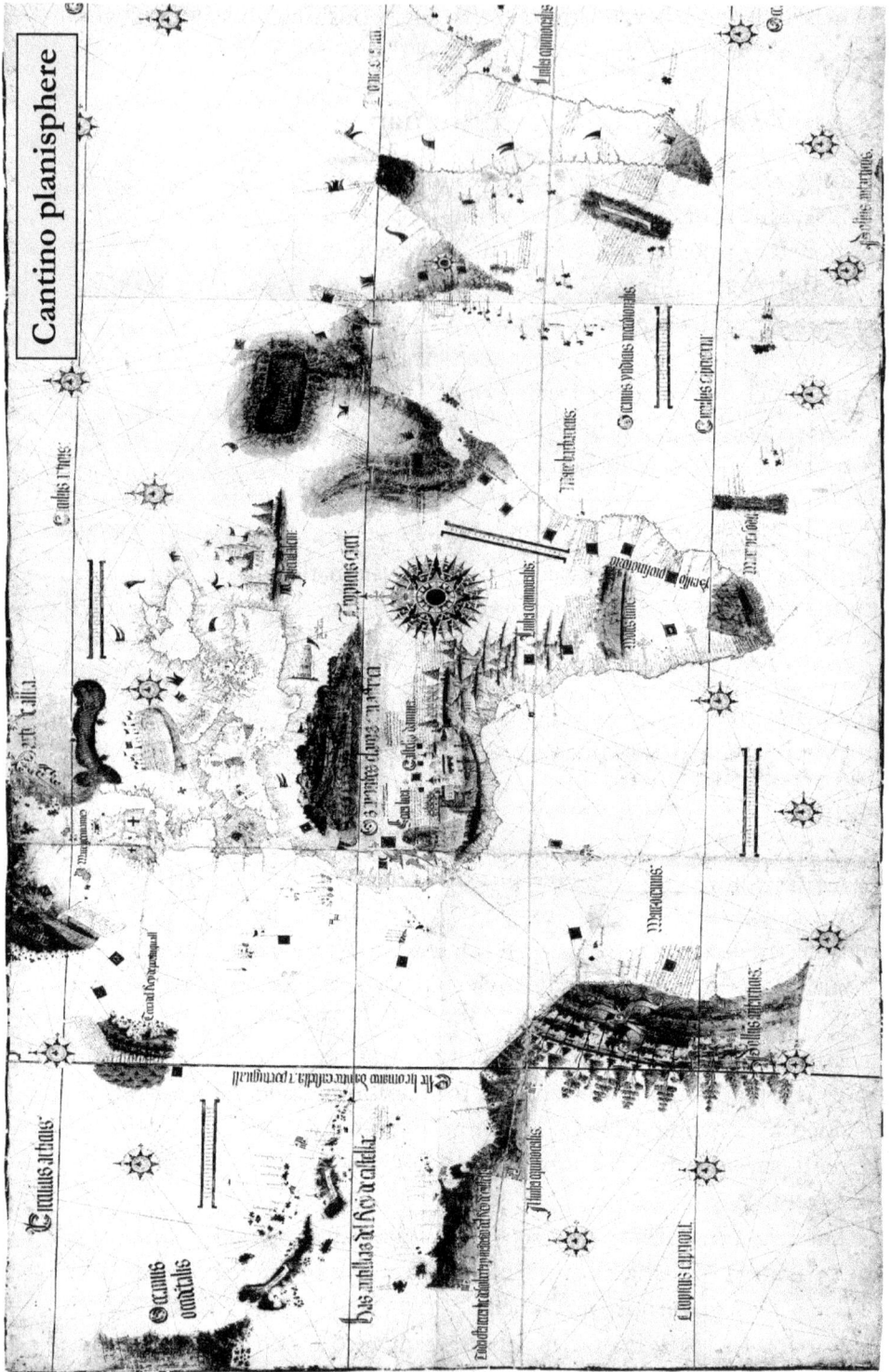

Cantino planisphere

seeing Balboa as an obstacle, had him arrested and tried for treason. In a biased trial, Balboa and four others were found guilty and beheaded.

The Cantino planisphere

The Cantino planisphere[3] (left) is the earliest-surviving map that shows Portuguese discoveries in Asia and South America up to 1500. The map is a guidebook to Europeans' voyages, its detail showing where they had ventured, and less or none where they had not.

The map shows considerable accuracy of both the west and east coasts of Africa, which by that time the Portuguese had explored. To the east beyond Africa detail fades, along the coast of India and into Asia. The map offers literally sketchy knowledge of the Malay Peninsula and Southeast Asia, and in the Americas to the south it ends suddenly in Brazil.

Magellan

Magellan's knowledge was a few steps ahead of the Cantino map, in Southeast Asia and in South America.

In Lisbon after his return, Magellan had access to the latest intelligence and reports coming in and there were a lot. Portugal was sending annual spice fleets to India as well as fleets to the South American coast to haul back brazilwood (hence the name Brazil). After relocating to Seville in 1518, Magellan continued to seek new reports there.

Like Columbus, however, Magellan underestimated the earth's size—he figured Asia lay just beyond his strait. It took his fleet not weeks as expected but three months to cross the Pacific Ocean, and they were making good time by their own reckoning.

Still, Magellan succeeded. Magellan led a fleet on the first European crossing of the ocean he named Mar Pacifico, and with the help of his pilot Francisco Albo charted for the first time a giant swatch of the earth that Europeans had yet to put on their maps.

Magellan proved the world was round not by circling it completely but simply by reaching Asia sailing westward instead of eastward—the proof found when Enrique of Malacca, Magellan's slave-interpreter, was able to converse with locals, likely in Malay, on Limasawa Island in the (modern-day) Philippines.

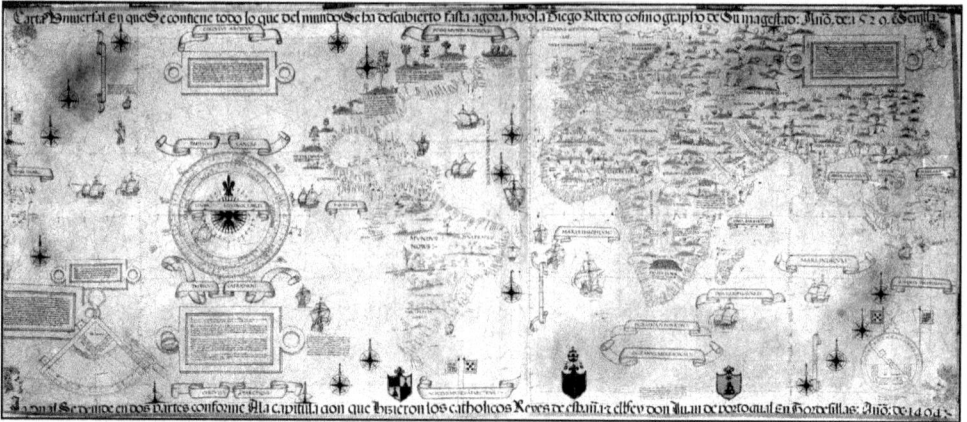

Diogo Ribeiro's 1529 world map (above) includes Magellan's discoveries. The Pacific Ocean, still unexplored, is largely blank, and the American continents simply fade into nothingness to the west, their coasts still uncharted.

This was new: Europeans were now leaving blank spots on their maps—they used to fill empty areas with pictures of legendary creatures and the like. The blank spots said "We don't know" and served as a beacon to people to explore and fill them in. And their exploring was more than about maps; they were collecting information on climate, flora, fauna, people, cultures, and languages.

Of course, the European explorations were different from anything before in one very important respect: The Europeans set out not just to discover but to conquer and colonize. Around the Indian Ocean, that meant the disruption of trade that had flourished for centuries as Europeans established control over whole areas of the planet. In the Americas it meant the destruction of empires and the annihilation and genocide of entire peoples.

The Renaissance had arrived, but the Europeans carried with them the culture of war that had dominated the continent for a millennium.

---

1. Cropping these maps and displaying them in grayscale as they are here is a crime against cartography. High-resolution and full-color images of all of these are available to view for free on Wikipedia and on other sites.

2. Two copies of the Fra Mauro map were produced; one remained in Venice.

3. Portugal guarded all knowledge of geography as a state secret. It was illegal to bring maps and documents on navigation out of the kingdom. The Cantino planisphere got its name from Alberton Cantino, who smuggled it from Portugal to Italy in 1502.

5.

Francisco Albo and His Navigational Log

A MONTH INTO MAGELLAN'S EXPEDITION, Francisco Albo[1] began a navigational log that he maintained continuously over the three-year voyage, rain or shine. While Pigafetta recorded the human side of the journey, Albo's log gives us a picture of the fleet's course and progress as it circled the world—and just a bit of detail beyond.

A native of Rhodes, Albo signed on as a master's mate aboard the flagship *Trinidad* and soon assumed the duties of pilot. It was about this time that he began his log.

After the massacre at Cebu, Albo was one of the few skilled mariners left. He was pilot of the *Victoria* and one of the eighteen crew members who returned to Seville in 1522, and one of three who reported to Charles V at Valladolid.

Importantly, Albo avoided the fleet's political controversies and concentrated on navigation, recording the fleet's position each day. His log is generally all business with few details beyond recording the course.

The outside details Albo occasionally offers give us a glimpse of the man's professional mindset. For instance, while Pigafetta left behind an R-rated account of the fleet's stopover in Brazil, Albo's main interest was in describing the bay and harbor, though he did add an affectionate sentence on the Tupi people who welcomed them.

> Passing the said cape there is a large bay, and at its entrance there is a low island, and the bay within is very large, with many ports; it extends two leagues from the mouth, and it is called Bay of St. Lucy; and if you wish to pass the island, you leave it on the left hand, and (the entrance) is narrow; but there is a depth of 7 fathoms, and a foul bottom ...

> In this bay there are good people, and plenty of them, and they go naked, and barter with fish-hooks, and looking-glasses, and little bells, for victuals. There is a good deal of brazil wood ...

Magellan and Elcano circumnavigation

20/09/1519–06/09/1522

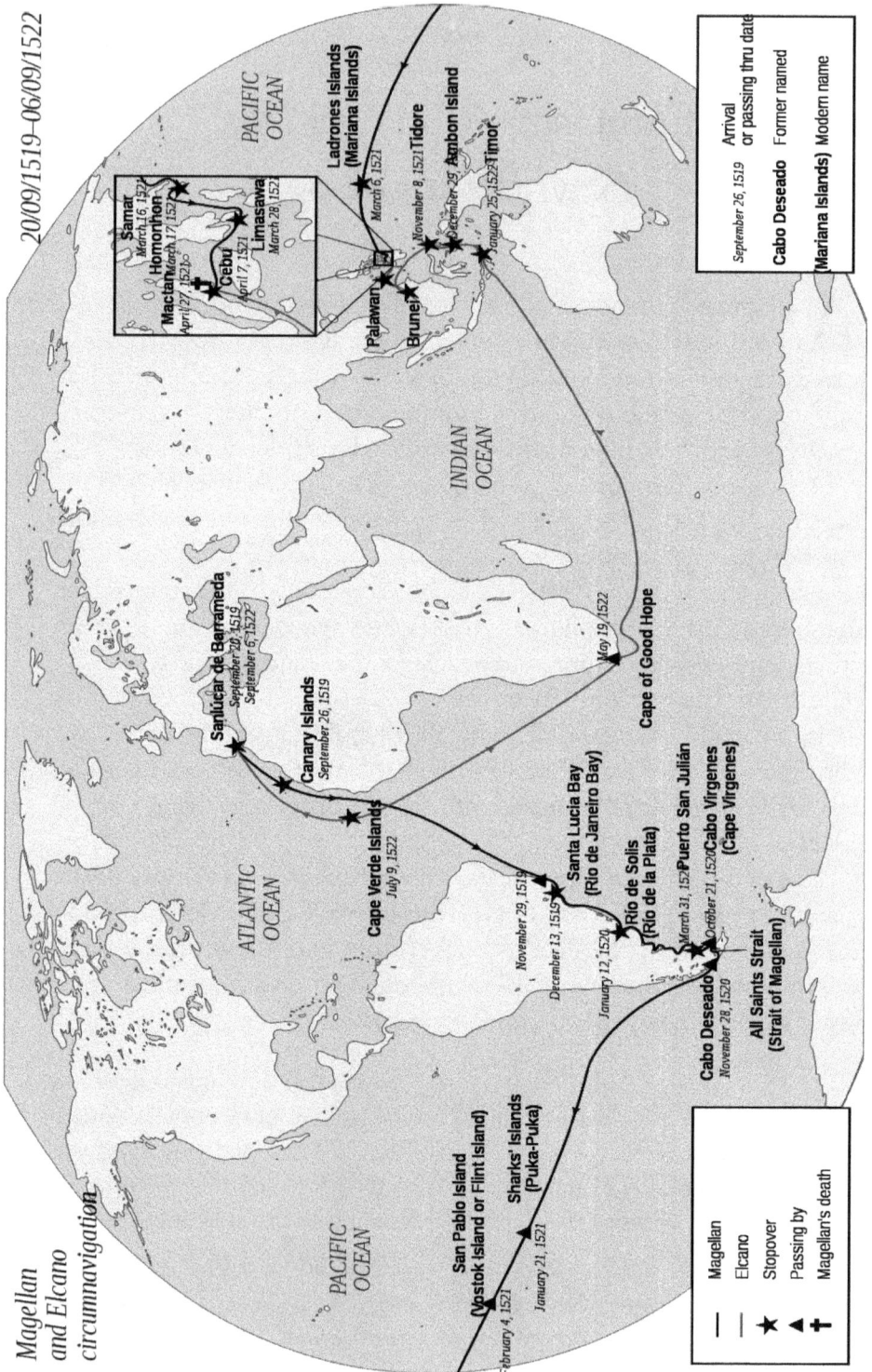

PACIFIC OCEAN

Ladrones Islands (Mariana Islands)
March 6, 1521

Tidore
November 8, 1521

Ambon Island
December 27

Timor
January 25, 1522

Samar
March 16, 1521
Homonhon
Limasawa
March 28, 1521
Cebu
April 7, 1521
Mactan
April 27, 1521

Palawan
Brunei

INDIAN OCEAN

May 19, 1522

Cape of Good Hope

Sanlúcar de Barrameda
September 20, 1519
September 6, 1522

Canary Islands
September 26, 1519

ATLANTIC OCEAN

Cape Verde Islands
July 9, 1522

Santa Lucia Bay
(Rio de Janeiro Bay)
November 29, 1519

Río de Solís
(Río de la Plata)
December 13, 1519

Puerto San Julián
March 31, 1520
January 12, 1520

Cabo Virgenes
(Cape Virgenes)
October 21, 1520

Cabo Deseado
November 28, 1520

All Saints Strait
(Strait of Magellan)

San Pablo Island
(Vostok Island or Flint Island)

Sharks' Islands
(Puka-Puka)
January 21, 1521

PACIFIC OCEAN

February 4, 1521

September 26, 1519	Arrival or passing thru date
Cabo Deseado	Former named
(Mariana Islands)	Modern name

—	Magellan
		Elcano
★	Stopover
◄	Passing by
✝	Magellan's death

At Puerto San Julián he wrote similarly of the Tehuelches.

> ... there we caulked the ships, and many Indians came there, who go covered with skins of antas [llamas], which are like camels without humps, and they carry some bows of canes very small like the Turkish, and the arrows are like theirs, and at the point they have a flint tip for iron, and they are very swift runners, and well made men, and well fashioned.

During the three-month Pacific crossing, Albo's log records only positions—there were no anchorings or land masses to discuss. The bleak daily records must have become surreal to Albo by month two or three, as crewmen lay suffering from scurvy and starving to death on deck—on what was appearing to be a hopeless journey.

Scurvy was a mysterious and deadly condition suffered on most long-distance sea voyages. Victims became lethargic and suffered bleeding of the skin, and their gums swelled up to the point they could no longer eat. Estimates have put the number of sailors killed by scurvy during the period as high as 2 million.

By 1500 the Portuguese came across the cure when an expedition led by Pedro Álvares Cabral reached Malindi, where lemons and oranges helped fight the condition. The dreaded disease turned out to be simply a vitamin C deficiency, a shipboard problem famously solved two and a half centuries later when James Cook circumnavigated the globe aboard the HMS *Endeavor*, loaded with sauerkraut for provisions. Not a single sailor died of scurvy on the voyage.

But scurvy wreaked havoc on Magellan's expedition.

After two months in the Pacific, the fleet chanced upon an isolated island, one that offered no safe anchoring, so they were forced to just sail by. In his log, Albo remained businesslike:

> And in this neighbourhood we found an islet with trees on it. It is uninhabited; and we took soundings at it, and found no bottom, and so we went on our course. We called this islet San Pablo, having discovered it on the day of his conversion, and it is ... leagues from that of Tiburones.

Ten days later they found another island and again could not anchor. So they continued for another three weeks before finally two larger islands appeared, the second one Guam.

By this time the ships had wandered for three months at sea without hope, they had sent the bodies of twenty-plus crewmen overboard to a burial at sea, and more lay sick and dying around them. And the welcome they received from the Chamorros on Guam was far from warm.

But that's not what Fransisco Albo focused on in his report. Albo was more interested in the Chamorros' impressive boats and skills on the water than he was in their attempt to carry away anything that was not nailed down, including Magellan's skiff:

> On the 6th (March), to W., in 13°. This day we saw land, and went to it, and there were two islands, which were not very large; and when we came between them, we turned to the S.W., and left one to the N.W., and then we saw a quantity of small sails coming to us, and they ran so, that they seemed to fly, and they had mat sails of a triangular shape, and they went both ways, for they made of the poop the prow, and of the prow the poop, as they wished, and they came many times to us and sought us to steal whatever they could; and so they stole the skiff of the flag-ship, and next day we recovered it ...

Only the last few phrases mention the incident that turned into a small battle the next day.[2]

Albo remained committed to his log as the fleet forged on, recording key details of Brunei and the Moluccas—the Spice Islands they were sent to explore—as well as the *Victoria*'s track across the Indian Ocean and around the Cape of Good Hope.

Finally, after three years of keeping records, Albo called it a day when the *Victoria* spotted Cape St. Vincent, a headland in Portugal.

September, 1522.

> On the 4th of the said month, in the morning, we saw land, and it was Cape St. Vincent, and it was to the north-east of us, and so we changed our course to the S.E., to get away from that Cape.

---

1. Francisco Albo (also Alvo, Calvo).

2. Historians have noted that the Chamorros on Guam had a different view of property and ownership.

6.

Cartagena and Mutiny at Puerto San Julián

Juan de Cartagena.

HISTORY LABELS the likes of Magellan and Columbus as "explorers" and "navigators," whereas Juan de Cartagena is remembered as an "accountant"—not quite the swashbuckling image that inspires fifth-grade history classes.

The *accountant* note was important, though—Cartagena was sent to watch Magellan and possibly depose him as captain-general along the journey. Cartagena is the villain in films and documentaries about Magellan's expedition. A bit of nepotism lifted Cartagena to No. 2 in the fleet and ultimately led to his isolated demise.

A native of Burgos, Cartagena was the original captain of the *San Antonio*, the largest and most expensive ship in the fleet.

When Spain's newly crowned King Charles agreed to back Magellan's expedition, Castilian officials at Valladolid quickly set out to undermine the project. The idea of a Portuguese commander of such a fleet was unthinkable. (Charles was a Habsburg from Flanders working with Flemish advisers.)

The day the Articles of Agreement for Magellan's expedition were signed, a royal decree was issued naming Cartagena as the armada's inspector-general—a clear check on Magellan's power. Cartagena was "nephew" of Archbishop Juan Rodríguez de Fonseca, *nephew* being a term widely understood to mean illegitimate son. Whatever the truth, it was a relationship other officers in the fleet knew of and one that Magellan was forced to respect, to a degree.

As Magellan's armada set out, it was divided into two main factions: the Portuguese and supernumeraries aboard the *Trinidad*, who would support Magallan, and the Castilian captains and officers of the *San Antonio*, the *Concepción*, and the *Victoria,* who were by no means trusted by their captain general.

Six days out the fleet reached the Canary Islands, where they stopped for water and wood. There, at Punta Rojo, a caravel from San Lúcar arrived with a message for Magellan. The message was from Diogo Barbosa, Magellan's father-in-law and a sponsor of sorts. It warned that the Castilian captains had been heard boasting of plans to mutiny and kill Magellan if needed.

The Castilians were only one of Magellan's concerns. He knew that Portuguese ships were likely sent to stop him. Fearing some of his own officers might pass information to them, Magellan filed one route plan but led the fleet on a different course.

The unannounced changes quickly brought criticism from Cartagena, who demanded answers.

Magellan coldly ignored him and continued silently for two weeks as the fleet headed south. When the fleet neared the Cape Verde Islands, they were hit by a series of tropical storms and found themselves surrounded by sharks, as well. "They have terrible teeth, and whenever they find men in the sea they devour them," Pigafetta wrote, adding, "We caught many of them with iron hooks, although they are not good to eat unless they are small ..."

At the height of one storm, lightning was seen behind the masts and the superstitious crew believed it was the manifestation of St. Elmo, the patron saint of mariners. As Pigafetta wrote, "When that blessed light was about to leave us, so dazzling was the brightness that it cast into our eyes, that we all remained for more than an eighth of

ATLANTIC
OCEAN
Sanlúcar de B
September 2
September 6
Canary Islands
September 26, 1519
Cape Verde Island
July 9, 1522
November 29, 151
December 13, 1519
Santa Lucia Bay
(Rio de Janeiro Bay)
January 12, 1520
Rio de Solis
(Rio de la Plata)
Cape of Go
March 31, 152 Puerto San Julián
Cabo Deseado   October 21, 1520 Cabo Virgenes
November 28, 1520   (Cape Virgenes)
All Saints Strait
(Strait of Magellan)

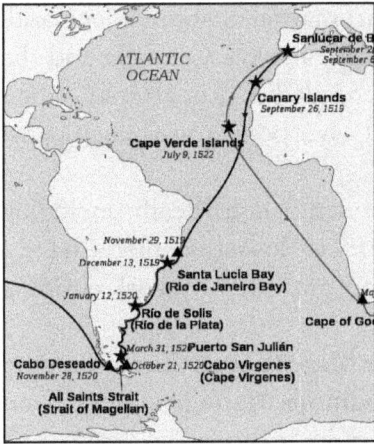

an hour blinded and calling for mercy. And truly when we thought that we were dead men, the sea suddenly grew calm."

As the storms subsided, however, the fleet entered the doldrums, an area of low pressure devoid of winds, where ships might float helplessly for weeks on end. The move seriously stalled the fleet's progress, though it was a course the Portuguese would never suspect.

Adding to the crew's discomfort, the stench of rotting provisions and bilgewater was rising up to deck, leaving no escape.

A showdown between Magellan and Cartagena was inevitable. It happened during a heated discussion aboard the *Trinidad*, where officers were questioning Magellan's course. Cartagena became openly defiant, prompting Magellan to arrest his inspector-general and put him in irons on the main deck.

Surrounded by armed guards, the other officers remained silent as Cartagena called openly for mutiny. Magellan gave custody of the prisoner to Luis de Mendoza, the *Victoria*'s captain.

Discontent among the crew eased certainly during their weeks in Brazil, but it returned soon after they set out. By April when they wintered at Puerto San Julián, another showdown was brewing, and this one would grow into outright mutiny.

On the night of April 1, 1520, Cartagena joined the *Concepción*'s Captain Gaspar de Quesada; its pilot, Juan Sebastián Elcano; and thirty Spanish crew members in boarding and seizing control of the *San Antonio*. Suddenly three ships—the *San Antonio*, the *Concepción*, and the *Victoria*—were pitted against Magellan's flagship *Trinidad* and the *Santiago*.

Magellan is remembered as an explorer and navigator, but at Puerto San Julián it was his military expertise that saved the expedition. Although outnumbered, Magellan quickly prevailed in a battle at sea that included sending Duarte Barbosa to board the *Victoria* and retake the ship by force, a decisive surprise attack that left Mendoza, its captain, dead.[1]

Magellan immediately convened a court martial onshore. Mendoza's body was propped up so he could be tried, as well. Quesada and the dead Mendoza were sentenced to be beheaded and quartered—their dismembered body parts were displayed on a pole, a warning against future revolt.

In all, forty crew members were condemned to death, including Elcano, though Magellan couldn't afford to lose that many hands. Instead he commuted their sentences and put them to work cleaning the bilges and working the pumps.

The fleet wintered in Patagonia, where Magellan had the crew empty and recondition the ships in icy cold conditions. Cartagena once again tried to incite a mutiny, but the plot was quickly exposed.

Exasperated, Magellan sentenced Cartagena and the *San Antonio*'s chaplain, Bernard Calmette,[2] who was involved, to be marooned.

On August 11, 1520, Juan de Cartagena and Calmette were brought to a small island in a longboat, where they were left with only their swords and a supply of sea biscuit and wine—this along a coastline where the fleet had already encountered cannibals and Patagonian "giants."

---

1. Read more about the mutiny in later chapters.

2. Bernard Calmette, historians believe, was the real name of the chaplain assigned to the *San Antonio* and marooned in Patagonia with Juan de Cartagena, following their attempted mutiny. Various records including Pigafetta's journal show the name Pero Sánchez or Paro Sánchez de la Reina. Calmette was a native of Lectoure in France.

7.

Paulo and the Patagonian Giants

Magellan's dancing Patagonian giant.

A S THEY SAILED off the map's end, beyond the point where the last explorers charting their way down the coast were killed and eaten by cannibals, Magellan's crew came across a naked giant dancing and singing along the shore.

The Roman author Pliny the Elder wrote of exotic creatures and strange humans that writers of medieval travelogues repeated and added to. These beings included people with a single eye in the middle of their forehead, humans with their feet turned backward, and men with dogs' heads.

When they met the Tehuelches, an indigenous people in Patagonia, their imaginations took over. Wrote Pigafetta:

> One day we suddenly saw a naked man of giant stature on the shore of the port, dancing, singing, and throwing dust on his head ... He was so tall that we reached only to his waist, and he was well proportioned.

His face was large and painted red all over while about his eyes he was painted yellow; and he had two hearts painted on the middle of his cheeks. His scanty hair was painted white. He was dressed in the skins of animals skillfully sewn together.

Detail from a map.

This was Europeans' first encounter with the people Magellan called the Patagons—the Patagonian giants, as the world came to know them. The tall tales of later expeditions made the Patagonians even taller— ten feet or more. Sir Francis Drake saw them on his voyage through the strait. His nephew wrote in *The World Encompassed*, in 1628:

> Magellan was not altogether deceived in naming these giants, for they generally differ from the common sort of man both in stature, bigness and strength of body, as also in the hideousness of their voices: but they are nothing so monstrous and giant-like as they were represented, there being some English men as tall as the highest we could see, but peradventure the Spaniards did not think that ever any English man would come hither to reprove them, and therefore might presume the more boldly to lie.

Reports of the giants sparked popular interest and the myth continued to grow well into the nineteenth century, when more-scientific reports brought the Patagonians' height down to size. It's likely that they were tall, six or seven feet, and statuesque, but they were being perceived by sixteenth-century Europeans who averaged just over five feet in height themselves.[1] And read fantastic stories that came from Pliny the Elder.

Meanwhile—no surprise—Antonio Pigafetta was there to record a first impression of the giants, of their customs and language—and, importantly, the Europeans' response to a Star Trek-like first contact moment:

> The captain-general sent one of our men to the giant so that he might perform the same actions as a sign of peace. Having done that, the man led the giant to an islet into the presence of the captain-general. When the giant was in the captain-general's and our presence, he marveled greatly and made signs with one finger raised upward, believing that we had come from the sky. . . .

The captain-general had the giant given something to eat and drink, and among other things which were shown to him was a large steel mirror. When he saw his face, he was greatly terrified, and jumped back throwing three or four of our men to the ground. After that he was given some bells, a mirror, a comb, and certain Pater Nosters. The captain-general sent him ashore with four armed men.

A Giant Named John

The fleet soon made contact with more of the Patagonians, including women. But the giants were wary of their visitors and kept a distance. One who was braver came to a small house the fleet built during their winter stopover for the smiths and for storage:

> That man was even taller and better built than the others and as tractable and amiable. Jumping up and down, he danced, and when he danced, at every leap, his feet sank a palmo into the earth. He remained with us for a considerable number of days, so long that we baptized him, calling him Johanni. He uttered [the words] "Jesu," "Pater Noster," "Ave Maria" and "Jovani."
>
> Then the captain-general gave him a shirt, a woolen jerkin [camisota de panno], cloth breeches, a cap, a mirror, a comb, bells, and other things, and sent him away like his companions. He left us very joyous and happy. The following day he brought one of those large animals to the captain-general, in return for which many things were given to him, so that he might bring some more to us; but we did not see him again.
>
> We thought that his companions had killed him because he had conversed with us.

Part of the explorer mindset, one quick reaction to meeting a novel new people was the urge to kidnap a few to bring home as a souvenir. On his return to Spain Columbus presented captured natives to Ferdinand and Isabella, and the Portuguese brought people back from East Africa and India.

With the Patagonians, however, capturing a few specimens was going to be no easy task. The giants easily outran the Europeans with their long strides, and they were far too large and strong to wrestle. But as Pigafetta explained, Magellan came up with a cruel but clever solution.

The captain-general kept two of them—the youngest and best proportioned—by means of a very cunning trick, in order to take them to Spagnia. Had he used any other means, they could easily have killed some of us.

The trick thát he employed in keeping them was as follows. He gave them many knives, scissors, mirrors, bells, and glass beads; and those two having their hands filled with the said articles, the captain-general had two pairs of iron manacles brought, such as are fastened on the feet.

He made motions that he would give them to the giants, whereat they were very pleased since those manacles were of iron, but they did not know how to carry them. They were grieved at leaving them behind, but they had no place to put those gifts; for they had to hold the skin wrapped about them with their hands. ... the captain made them a sign that he would put them on their feet, and that they could carry them away. They nodded assent with the head. Immediately, the captain had the manacles put on both of them at the same time. ...

When they saw later that they were tricked, they raged like bulls, calling loudly for Setebos to aid them. ...

It's worth noting that Pigafetta was one member of Magellan's crew who took a genuine interest in the local peoples they met, yet even he showed no remorse in kidnapping two men and taking them away.

Unlikely Patagonian Explorers

Magellan and his crew captured two of Tehuelches and put them in irons to be brought back to King Charles. Both died at sea, one in the Atlantic, one in the Pacific.

It's a wonder what must have been going through their minds. These strange beings (the Europeans) had come from the sky in giant boats and now were whisking the giants away. To where and for what purpose?

The Patagonian that Pigafetta got to know aboard the *Trinidad* made that first wondrous journey through Magellan's strait. He would have witnessed the mysterious views of white, jagged peaks and rocky coves along with the crew. Was this a magical river that led into the sky, to the end of Earth and life as the giant had known it?

A 1904 photo of a group of Tehuelches in Argentina.

His European shipmates would have viewed the strait with equal wonder. They had left the world they'd known, as it was known, sailed well beyond the end of all maps even before meeting their giant. To them the passage may also have seemed like a river to the afterlife, and for many it was.

Soon they entered a new ocean, one so utterly calm that Magellan dubbed it the Pacific sea. Still waters and a miracle wind at their back sent them speeding into the unknown fast, but where they expected to find island paradises rich in spices and wealth they found only endless open waters that each day cast an image of ever-greater isolation and gloom.

The Tehuelche would have witnessed many of Magellan's crew lose hope as impending death, starvation, and scurvy replaced thoughts of a world left behind. As he contemplated his own unlikely end, the giant would have seen these godlike Europeans face their own.

Were these minor demons, *Cheleule*, that the giant found himself among, since they suffered and died just like people?

As Pigafetta wrote, "this malady was the worst, namely that the gums of most part of our men swelled above and below so that they could not eat. And in this way they died, inasmuch as twenty-nine of us died, and the other giant died, and an Indian of the said country of Verzin [Rio]."

Pigafetta noted that those refusing to eat rats were among the first to die. He had already mentioned that the Patagonian on the *Trinidad* ate rats without even skinning them first, so the giant likely lasted for some time.

Here is Pigafetta's account of the captured Patagonian's end:

> Once I made the sign of the cross, and, showing it to him, kissed it. He immediately cried out "Setebos" [great god] and made me a sign that if I made the sign of the cross again, Setebos would enter into my body and cause it to burst.

> When that giant was sick, he asked for the cross, and embracing it and kissing it many times, desired to become a Christian before his death. We called him Paulo.

Paulo had been kidnapped by strange men—only men, why no women?—and chained up in their large black ship ... where a man who sounded different from the rest constantly pestered him to learn what he called things, where they gathered around to cheer and watch him eat, where around them in every direction was nothing but water, where the strange men fell ill, their mouths swollen up so they could not talk or eat, as he too became weak and hungry as the foreigners no longer brought him food, could no longer care for him ... and possibly one odd final thought for a Patagonian native in the winter of 1521 as he succumbed to death in the middle of Pacific Ocean: "And they called me Paulo."

---

1. The comedian Kevin Hart, a talented basketball player featured in NBA celebrity all-star games, has posed for pictures beside the NBA's tallest. Standing alongside NBA great Yao Ming, Hart appears as the Europeans would have viewed themselves next to the "giants" of Patagonia.

8.

Juan Serrano and the
Santiago Shipwreck

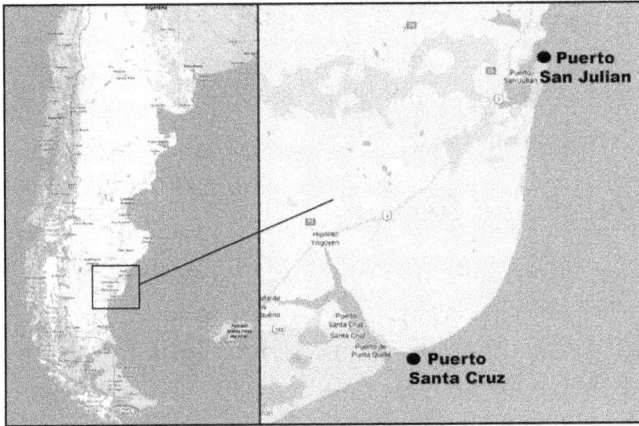

OF THE SHIPS' CAPTAINS, Juan Rodríguez Serrano was the most valuable to Magellan. Serrano was the only original captain who remained loyal during the mutiny at Puerto San Julián, and his skills as a mariner helped save lives and navigate the strait.

It's uncertain whether Serrano was Spanish or Portuguese. Some historians believe he was João Rodrigues Serrão, brother of Francisco Serrão, Magellan's close friend who reached the Spice Islands from Malacca a decade earlier. If so, he may have been a friend in India of Duarte Barbosa's, Magellan's brother-in-law, who like Magellan relocated from Portugal to Seville.

Whatever his origin, Serrano had sailed aboard Spanish ships since his youth and had crossed the Atlantic twice before, to the coast of Brazil in 1499–1500 and to Darién in 1514. A royal pilot, Serrano joined Magellan's fleet as captain and pilot of the *Santiago*, the smallest of the five ships. Sailing with him were his stepson, Francisco, and a black slave named Juan.

At Puerto San Julián, Magellan found himself facing three of the five ships in the Easter mutiny. When he checked on the one remaining ship, the *Santiago*, he found that Serrano remained loyal. Had Serrano sided with the mutineers, the name Magellan might well be unknown today.

Serrano's skills as a pilot proved indispensable. After the mutiny, Magellan had the ships emptied and reconditioned. The *Santiago* was the first ship ready to sail, and anxious to get the expedition moving, Magellan sent it ahead to scout the coast, to seek either a strait or a cape—or at least a better place to replenish supplies.

The *Santiago* left Puerto San Julián around May 1, and on May 6 found an estuary full of seals and penguins. Serrano named the estuary Santa Cruz. He kept the ship there for two weeks while the crew slaughtered and roasted seals.

Shipwreck and Rescue

Shortly after departing on May 22, the *Santiago* was hit by a fierce storm. Winds tore away its sails and a large wave washed away its rudder, leaving the *Santiago* floating helplessly, the storm driving it toward shore.

Here, Serrano's experience came to the rescue. The royal pilot managed to hoist a spare sail and—with no rudder—steer the ship bow first toward a beach. Hitting rocks would have meant disaster, yet Serrano brought the *Santiago* to rest close enough to sand that all but one crew member were able to jump to safety.

Minutes later the *Santiago* broke up in the waves. Serrano's slave, Juan, was the only man not to make it.

The ship's crew found themselves stranded far beyond the end of the map, in winter conditions and with little food. Making matters more uncomfortable, they knew the map ended where it did because a landing party from the previous expedition down the coast was attacked *and eaten* by cannibals—with fellow crew looking on from offshore. That was the expedition of Juan Díaz de Solís, who reached and named Rio de la Plata, and it was Solís and a landing party who were killed (and eaten), bringing the expedition to an end.

With these bleak thoughts in mind Serrano led the group of thirty men over rough terrain for four days to return to the estuary. There they sent two young crewmen on, for a trek that took them nearly two weeks to reach Puerto San Julián, where the fleet waited.

Magellan sent a rescue party of twenty men on foot—loaded with bread and wine for the *Santiago*'s shipwrecked crew. It was June 26 when the rescue party arrived at Santa Cruz, some five weeks after the ill-fated *Santiago*'s shipwreck. Serrano's crew had been surviving in the open wilderness all that time.

Magellan reassigned Serrano as captain of the *Concepción*, whose original captain, Gaspar de Quesada, was executed following the mutiny.

Serrano's seamanship came in handy again just down the coast when Magellan found the inlet that turned out to be his strait. Magellan first sent the *Concepción* and *San Antonio* in to explore, when a storm suddenly hit, forcing the other three ships to sail back out of the bay. Inside the strait the *Concepción* and *San Antonio* struggled to avoid being driven into shore and were not seen again for two days. Again, Serrano's skills helped save the fleet.

After Magellan's death on April 27, 1521, Serrano and Barbosa were elected to replace him. Their tenure as commandeers was to be brief.[1]

---

1. Continued in later chapters.

9.

Joãozito Lopes Carvalho: First Native of Brazil to Cross the Pacific

Depiction of Cabral's first landing on the Island of the True Cross, Oscar Pereira da Silva (1904).

FERDINAND MAGELLAN'S EXPEDITION swept up several unlikely travelers along the way, among them a seven-year-old boy at Guanabara Bay (Rio de Janeiro). Half-Portuguese, half-Tupi Indian, the boy is remembered in history as Joãozito Lopes Carvalho. Young Joãozito became the first native of Brazil to cross the Pacific Ocean—on a year-and-a-half journey that for him ended at Brunei in 1521.

Joãozito was the son of João de Lopes Carvalho and a Tupi woman in what today is Rio de Janeiro. A Portuguese pilot, João Carvalho had traveled to Guanabara Bay in 1512 on the *Bertoa*, a commercial vessel sent to pick up dyewood there. Twelve years earlier a Portuguese expedition had stumbled upon the Brazilian coast en route to India and came across Guanabara on January 1, 1502. Thinking the bay was the mouth of a river, they named it Rio de Janeiro.

After his 1512 journey, Carvalho stayed behind for four years, possibly to manage a storage facility. During that time, he took a native mistress and apparently fathered the child.

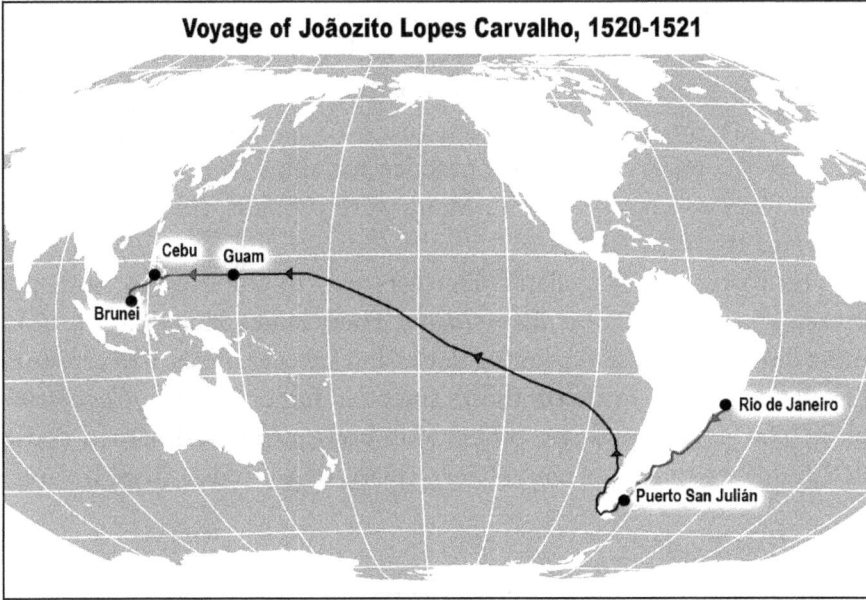

Voyage of Joãozito Lopes Carvalho, 1520-1521

Carvalho returned to Portugal in 1517, where his experience along the Brazilian coast caught Magellan's attention. He accompanied Magellan from Lisbon to Spain and was Magellan's original choice for captain of the *Santiago*, although Spanish officials objected because Carvalho was Portuguese.

Instead, Carvalho was made pilot of the *Concepción*, a 90-ton vessel whose 45-man crew included Captain Gaspar de Quesada and ship's master Juan Sebastián Elcano. Quesada became a leader of the failed Easter mutiny in April 1520 and was executed—beheaded and quartered—shortly after. Elcano survived the mutiny and later became captain of the *Victoria* and led the completion of the famed circumnavigation, bringing the ship back to Seville.

As Magellan's fleet neared the South American coast, Carvalho assured the Captain General that Guanabara Bay was a safe place to stop for provisions, where friendly natives would provide the fleet with fruits, vegetables, fish, and game.

Carvalho may also have been eager to visit the friendly women of Guanabara, who mixed readily with the Europeans—which would create problems for Magellan. One can imagine Carvalho exciting lonely sailors on deck with tales of the tropical paradise where "they go naked, both men and women," as Magellan's chronicler, Antonio Pigafetta, wrote.

Shortly after the fleet arrived at Guanabara, Carvalho's mistress appeared and presented the seven-year-old boy. Carvalho acknowledged the child as his and took Joãozito aboard the *Concepción* as a cabin boy.

It's hard to imagine what a seven-year-old was expected to contribute on such a voyage, but it was a practice for ships to bring along child pages, some as young as eight. Many were orphans, some were taken on board from the streets.

The roster for Magellan's fleet lists two to three cabin boys per vessel, with only one on the *Victoria*. Their duties included the tasks most disliked, such as scrubbing decks and serving meals. Joãozito may have been spared some of these, since his father was the *Concepción*'s pilot. The ship carried two other cabin boys, a Castilian named Pedro de Chindarza and a boy named Sean (Juan) Irés, listed as from Ireland.[1]

Paradise Lost

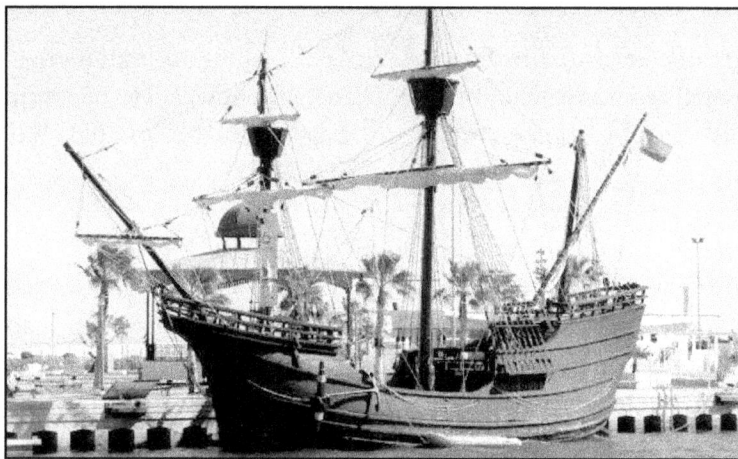

Replica of the *Victoria*, which was slightly smaller than the *Concepción*.

Boarding the *Concepción* must have been traumatic for a seven-year-old who had grown up in airy huts and spent much of his life outdoors in a land of plenty. The stench alone would have been unbearable. When the Spaniards arrived in Central America, the Aztecs escorted them around bearing incense burners. The newcomers saw this as a grand gesture of honor, but in fact the locals found the Spaniards' odor intolerable.

Aboard ship the human stench would have been worse. At sea, bathing was difficult, and when crew did bathe, it meant washing with saltwater that irritated skin and left them scratching.

The *Concepción* carried a crew of 45 men packed into the vessel's tight confines, competing for space with cargo, provisions, livestock, and at one point ("crammed with") strange-looking, flightless black "geese" found on an island—the first penguins most of the crew had ever seen ("… they were so fat that we didn't pluck them but skinned them …").

Then there were nonhuman smells: the stench of bilgewater rising from the hull, livestock, the slaughtering of livestock, and, as Pigafetta recorded, a note of rat urine.

And penguins.

Equally troubling would have been the food. Joãozito had grown up in a land abundant in fruit, fish, and wildlife. By contrast, the Spanish and Portuguese on land had a diet of meats loaded with perplexing combinations of spices, and coarse breads to chase that down. At sea, as soon as fresh provisions ran out—like penguin—fare would have been dried fish, sea biscuit, and whatever various crew cooked up from time to time.

What's more, for young Joãozito there was no one to complain *to* about such horrors, and no language to complain *in*. As quickly as many children pick up second languages, it's unlikely Joãozito learned much Portuguese from his father in the few weeks at Guanabara, and aboard the *Concepción*, the common language was Spanish. The majority of the crew were Castilian, along with a couple of gunners from Flanders, two Irish, a Genoese, and a sailor from Greece. Carvalho Sr. was one of seven Portuguese aboard.

Thus during the first weeks at sea, Joãozito's main means of communication would have been facial expressions and gestures. Grimacing at the constant stench and shoddy fare would have been an early language lesson. Beyond that for Joãozito Lopes Carvalho, learning survival Spanish literally meant survival.

Puerto San Julián, the Strait, and the Pacific

As the fleet set out, young Joãozito was well out of his element. It wasn't just shipboard routine he had to learn. Joãozito was speaking new languages, eating new foods, and wearing clothes for the first time—life on board would have been too cold not to. And all the while he had to deal with the ship constantly pitching and rolling on the waves.

For introduction, the fleet sailed into several months of increasingly bad weather. Late one night a midnight gale stretched into a three-day storm so severe, it blew away the forecastles of all five ships and damaged their sterncastles. During that storm Joãozito witnessed the religious side of the Europeans' culture as terrified sailors all around him fervently shouted prayers and pledged to make pilgrimages—as Pigafetta noted.

The people at Guanabara reasoned the Europeans might be gods. "It had been about two months since it had rained in that land," Pigafetta wrote, "and when we reached that port, it happened to rain, whereupon they said that we came from the sky and that we had brought the rain with us."[2]

A short way out to sea, Joãozito saw these strangers calling to their own gods for salvation.

With winter coming on, the fleet found refuge from the weather at the bay Magellan named Puerto San Julián, but things were far from calm. This was the first

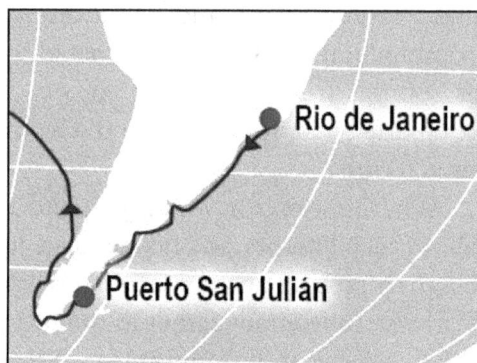

place away from home where young Joãozito spent enough time to build a lasting impression, and a strong one it would be.

Once the ships were anchored, Magellan cut rations, causing outrage among crew and officers alike and crushing what morale remained. Here, Joãozito saw the angry side of this cold culture and probably learned some of its nastier language as well.

Joãozito sailed aboard the *Concepción*, one of three ships caught up in the Easter mutiny that followed. No fighting took place on the *Concepción*, but its captain, Gaspar de Quesada, was one of the officers who headed the revolt. This was a man Joãozito would have seen regularly on deck, the man all crew kept an eye out for.

A week after the mutiny and a court martial, Quesada was beheaded by his own squire. His body and the body of Luis de Mendoza, *Victoria's* captain, were quartered, their dismembered body parts displayed on a pole as a warning—one all crew would have viewed at least from a distance.

Down the coast from Puerto San Julián, the fleet found an inlet, a possible strait. Magellan sent the *Concepción* and *San Antonio* in to explore, and almost immediately a severe storm hit. The two ships were separated and seemingly lost, young Joãozito with them.

"We thought that they had been wrecked, first, by reason of the violent storm, and second, because two days had passed and they had not appeared ..." Pigafetta wrote.

Then came a dramatic reunion. The *Concepción* and *San Antonio* appeared with pennants flying, crews cheering, and gunners firing salutes. They had returned and returned with news: The inlet was the strait they had been searching for.

But with victory in their grasp, the *San Antonio*, carrying a large portion of their remaining provisions, deserted and hightailed it back to Spain. Still, Magellan pressed on.

Joãozito witnessed that first trip through the strait's magical landscape, its dense forests, strange plants, and sharp white peaks creating a "deathlike scene of desolation," as Charles Darwin later wrote. Joãozito again saw the crew overcome with a collective emotion, this time wonder.

On November 28, 1520, the remaining three ships of the fleet entered the Pacific, an event that had the crew as elated as terrified. This was the unknown South Sea that Balboa had found. It's unlikely Joãozito understood the gravity of the moment, but he would have picked up on the excitement around him. They had sailed south well off the map and were now sailing north into the unknown ocean.

For two weeks the ships skirted the coast, making a first-ever tour along the southwestern shore of Chile. On December 15, 1520, they

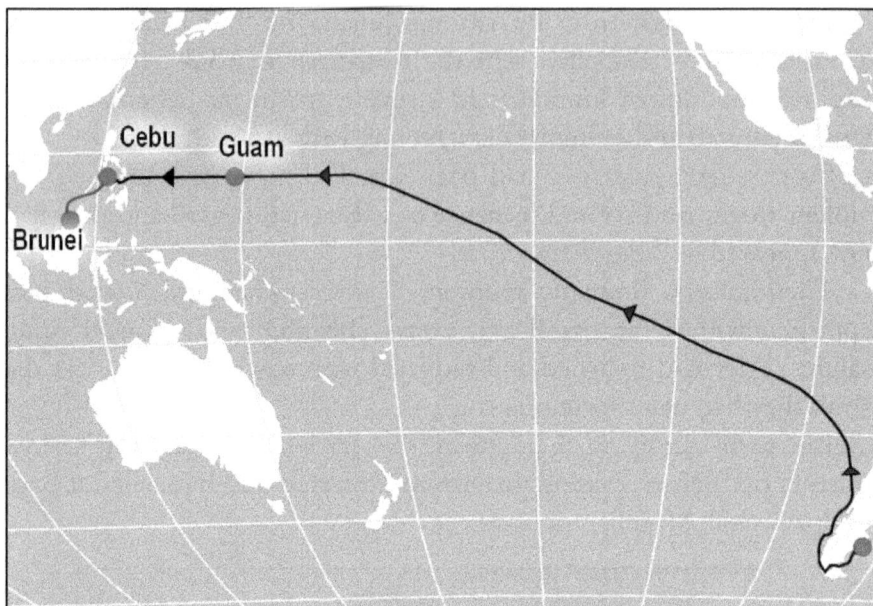

veered northwest, leaving behind the continent they had just begun charting—and Joãozito's home.

The three months that followed certainly had the biggest impression on Joãozito. Magellan expected Asia to be a short way out, and strong winds on a "pacifico" sea quickly put a return out of reach. They could only push on, day after day, wondering why no land was sighted.

The fleet spent over three months at sea. Some thirty men died of scurvy and starvation, and another thirty fell ill.

"We ate ... powder of biscuits swarming with worms, for they had eaten the good. It stank strongly of the urine of rats. We drank yellow water that had been putrid for many days," Pigafetta wrote. They also chewed on oxhide and ate any rats they could catch.

"But above all the other misfortunes the following was the worst. The gums of both the lower and upper teeth of some of our men swelled, so that they could not eat under any circumstances and therefore died."

Joãozito would have witnessed the mighty strangers sick and dying on deck around him—he may have been put to work caring for some.

Among the dead were two other South American natives—another Indian from Brazil and one of the two Patagonian giants the fleet had captured. The other died crossing the Atlantic on the San Antonio.

Joãozito, however, survived. Possibly his father, as the *Concepción*'s pilot, possessed or was able to get extra provisions.

In any case, Joãozito Lopes Carvalho became the first native of Brazil to cross the Pacific and visit East Asia. He was with the fleet as it stopped at Guam, Limasawa, Cebu, and eventually Brunei.

Cebu, Mactan, and Pirating in Brunei

After joining Magellan's fleet, Joãozito saw the crew shift collectively from one emotional state to another—terror in initial storms, fury leading up the Easter mutiny, wonder traversing the strait, and starvation and utter despair crossing the Pacific.

Then in the Philippines in April 1521, the fleet fell apart. Its backbone and driving force, Magellan, was killed in battle at the island of Mactan, and four days later most of its officers and pilots were slaughtered in an ambush at Cebu—among them the two officers elected to replace Magellan: Duarte Barbosa and Juan Serrano.

Joãozito's father, João de Lopes Carvalho, went ashore with the group, but at the last minute he and another officer, Gonzalo Gómez de Espinosa, became suspicious and fled back to the ships in a longboat. Just as they arrived, they heard shouts from beyond the beach. The captains and officers who went ashore were being killed as they listened. Apparently only Serrano and Magellan's slave, Enrique, were spared. Serrano was brought to the beach, beaten, and used as a hostage.

That left Joãozito's father as one of the only senior officers, and according to one account, on Carvalho's orders, they abandoned a weeping Serrano on the beach and set sail. Others have suggested Serrano ordered Carvalho to depart.

With Magellan, Barbosa, and Serrano gone, Carvalho was elected captain-general (and captain of the *Trinidad*), even though he was outranked by the *Concepción*'s master, Juan Sebastían Elcano. It was a choice that proved regrettable for the fleet and disastrous for Joãozito.

With too few men left to sail all three ships, they scuttled the *Concepción*, the ship in the worst condition, burning it so as to leave no monument behind. Carvalho began as pilot of the *Concepción*. Joãozito presumably transferred from that ship to the *Trinidad* with his father.

With Carvalho in command, the two remaining ships turned into a pirate fleet for a time, capturing and plundering local craft as they went. They wandered for several days to find provisions before kidnapping two Muslim pilots who could guide them to Brunei. These were tactics that Vasco da Gama and, shortly after, Pedro Álvares Cabral, adopted during the first Portuguese forays into India: capturing ships, holding hostages, and forcing local pilots to guide them.

And like da Gama and Cabral along the Indian coast, the fleet was sailing into a cultural unknown. As they entered the port of Brunei, they found a harbor bustling with traffic, a commercial center bigger and more advanced than anything they'd seen since leaving Europe. They would also, like da Gama and Cabral in Calicut, face a powerful local leader in Brunei's sultan.

Drawing depicting Brunei as the fleet arrived.

Antonio Pigafetta wrote a detailed description of Brunei, a city of buildings perched on poles:

> That city is entirely built in saltwater, except the houses of the king and certain chiefs. It contains twenty-five thousand fires [i.e., families]. The houses are all constructed of wood and built up from the ground on tall pillars. When the tide is high the women go in boats through the settlement selling the articles necessary to maintain life.
>
> There is a large brick wall in front of the king's house with towers like a fort, in which were mounted fifty-six bronze pieces, and six of iron. During the two days of our stay there, many pieces were discharged.

That king is a Moro and his name is Raia Siripada. He was forty years old and corpulent. No one serves him except women who are the daughters of chiefs. He never goes outside of his palace, unless when he goes hunting, and no one is allowed to talk with him except through the speaking tube.

As at Cebu, word of Portuguese attacks in India and Malacca had preceded the Spanish fleet. Possibly with a hint of irony, the visitors assured the Sultan that they were Spanish, not Portuguese, though the fleet's commander, Joãozito's father, was Portuguese, as was Magellan before him. And both Carvalho Sr. and Magellan had previously served the Portuguese king—Magellan at the sack of Malacca.

The fleet was allowed to stay at Brunei and trade for a few weeks, but tensions were constant. The Portuguese historian Gaspar Corrêa told the story in his *Lendas da Índia* (Legends of India, early 1500s):

> Carvalhinho became suspicious ... and ordered good watch to be kept day and night, and did not allow more than one or two men to go ashore. The king [sultan] perceiving this sent to beg Carvalhinho to send him his son who had brought the present, because his little children who had seen him, were crying to see him. He sent him, very well dressed, with four men, who, on arriving where the king was, were ordered by him to be arrested.

On July 29, the Spanish ships were approached by a fleet of two hundred pirogues and a battle ensued. The Spanish cannon quickly broke up the attack and the fleet moved to safety. The following day they captured a grounded junk and took sixteen hostages, among them a prince from Luzon and three women.

The plan was to ransom the prince and take the women back to Spain to present to the queen. But Carvalho Sr. instead took the women to his cabin as a personal harem, and made a secret deal with the Luzon prince, letting him escape for a sum of gold. Both moves outraged the crew and soon led to Carvalho's ouster as commander.

As for Joãozito, Pigafetta wrote:

> We sent a message to the king [sultan], asking him to please allow two of our men who were in the city for purposes of trade and the son of João Carvalho, who had been born in the country of Verzin [Brazil], to come to us, but the king refused. That was the consequences of João Carvalho letting the above captain [prince] go. We kept sixteen of the

chiefest men [of the captured junks] to take them to Spagnia, and three women in the queen's name, but João Carvalho usurped the latter for himself.

The fleet waited several days for the return of Joãozito and the others but finally departed. Here, Joãozito Carvalho, first native of Brazil to cross the Pacific, disappears from history at the age of eight or nine.

Whatever his fate, he faced inconceivable challenges.

In the year and a half Joãozito spent traveling from Rio to Brunei, he would have become at least functionally bilingual and possibly trilingual. Kids pick up languages fast, and at seven he was stripped from his village and brought to sea. Spanish was the main language of the fleet, and Carvalho Sr. was Portuguese, one of seven in the crew. And given the (sometimes) boredom of life at sea, Joãozito might have wondered also at the speech of the *Concepción*'s two gunners from Flanders or the two young crewmates from Ireland.

Now Joãozito found himself in the Sultanate of Brunei, in a multilingual port city where no one spoke any of the languages he knew. When Joãozito joined Magellan's fleet, daily survival depended on learning Spanish, just to find food and basic necessities. He had survived that test, but in Brunei, young Joãozito was starting all over.

A final thought, if Joãozito did live, did he grow up with any understanding of where he was from or appreciate the feat of having crossed the Pacific? What memories did he retain? Even in the royal household at Brunei, they may not have truly understood how the Spanish had traveled there, or what land young Joãozito had come from.

---

1. Of the other cabin boys on the *Concepción*, Sean (Juan) Irés was one of two Irish crew members. The other, William Irés, an apprentice seaman, may have been a brother. William Irés drowned at Rio de la Plata (near modern-day Buenos Aires) on Jan. 25, 1520. Sean Irés wound up on the *Trinidad* after the *Concepción* was scuttled. He died in October 1522. The other cabin boy on the *Concepción* was a Castilian named Pedro de Chindarza, who eventually made it back to Spain, in 1523, after being held for a time in the Cape Verde Islands.

2. Pigafetta added that their "simplicity" would make them easy Christian converts, which on reflection was not necessarily a compliment for his religion or mission. Pêro Vaz de Caminha made a similar observation there when the Portuguese first reached the area.

10.

Duarte Barbosa and Portuguese India

A relation of Ferdinand Magellan's by marriage, Duarte Barbosa was a key ally on Magellan's expedition, yet also a source of trouble more than once.[1] He may also have been among the experienced travelers in the crew, possibly having met Magellan in India around 1512.

Historians originally believed Barbosa was the author of a travel manuscript

Duarte Barbosa.

on East Africa, India, and beyond, *The Book of Duarte Barbosa*. The British historian Henry E. J. Stanley translated an Italian version of the manuscript in about 1874 and credited Magellan's Barbosa for the book, which was a colonial travel guide of sorts. [2] In his introduction Stanley added that Magellan may have contributed to parts.

In about 1920, Mansel Longworth Dames translated into English a Portuguese version and added a brief history of Barbosa as an introduction. According to Dames, Barbosa served for fifteen years in India, much of it in Cannanore (Kannur) where he worked as a scrivener at a Portuguese trading post. There he became fluent in Malayalam, an Indian language spoken around Kerala.

Historians have also speculated that Duarte Barbosa book may have been among the documents Magellan presented to King Charles when proposing his expedition. It reads like a brochure designed to sell a monarch on a colonial expedition, detailing riches and the new Portuguese trade.

Dames suggested that had Barbosa survived, he might have written his own account of the voyage, rivaling Antonio Pigafetta's journal.[3]

More recent studies, however, show that Barbosa the writer was likely not Magellan's relation. Records show three Duarte Barbosas in India at the time, and studies of the original Portuguese manuscript aim to one of the others.[4]

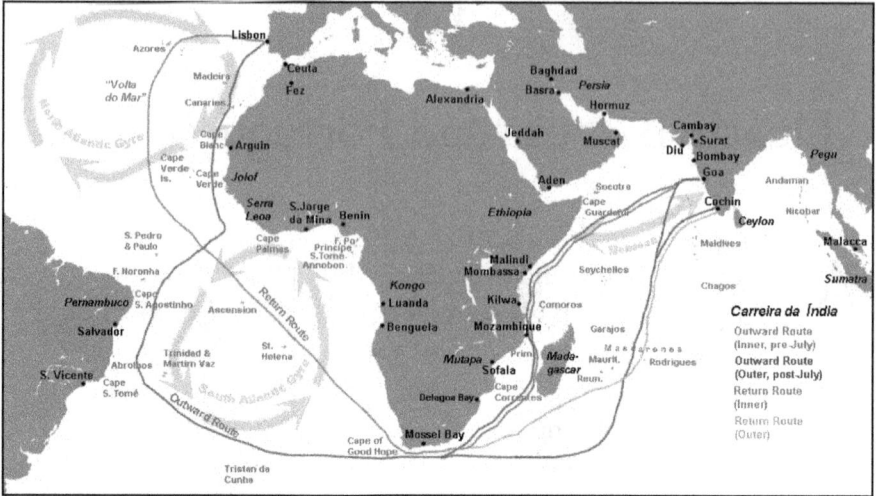

Portuguese trade routes around Africa and India. Note on the outward route, fleets sailed well into the Atlantic, nearing Brazil, to catch the trade winds.

Barbosa in India

Duarte Barbosa was born in Lisbon sometime around 1480 and sailed with the second or third Portuguese fleet to India. The accounts in his book suggest he traveled with the second, commanded by Pedro Álvares Cabral, the expedition that accidentally "discovered" the Brazilian coast. If so, Barbosa's stopover in Brazil with Magellan was a return visit.

Dames reported that Barbosa's father and uncle sailed with those early Portuguese fleets, and Duarte stayed behind with his uncle in Cochin (Kochi) and later transferred to Cannanore, where he worked in the Portuguese factory (trading post) in that city. A decade later, Portugal's viceroy Afonso de Albuquerque used a Duarte Barbosa as an interpreter in a 1514 meeting with Cochin's raja, where Albuquerque tried to persuade the raja to convert to Christianity.

Dames said Barbosa was among a group of colonists opposed to Albuquerque's plans for India, which sought to occupy and use Goa as Portugal's main India outpost—at the expense of already-established bases (and relationships) at Cochin and Cannanore. Barbosa's opposition to Albuquerque may have led to his being passed over for a top writer's position at Cannanore. Whatever the cause, Barbosa soon returned to Portugal and then, following his father, went to Seville in 1518.

By 1519, Portugal's empire spanned from Brazil to West Africa, India, and Malacca, held together by a series of forts and regular visits by fleets. Portugal upended centuries of trade across the India Ocean and Southeast Asia.

Duarte Barbosa's Colonial Travel Guide

Whoever the author, *The Book of Duarte Barbosa* provides valuable insight into the Portuguese mindset and budding Indian Ocean trade empire.

Barbosa's book is basically a colonial travel guide introducing cities and kingdoms and the various goods they traded in. The writer starts up the East Coast of Africa and moves on to India and beyond. His accounts show an enthusiastic interest in peoples and cultures in India, but the overwhelming impression is its callous outlook on Portuguese excesses.

The Portuguese sailed with orders to "discover" places in Africa and India and where possible wage war on and kill "Moors" (Muslims). Beginning with Vasco da Gama's first tour up the African coast, the Portuguese responded to all resistance with cannon fire and far worse —details Barbosa took very much in stride.

Stanley, who translated versions of both Barbosa's and Pigafetta's manuscripts, commented on this outlook in his introduction to Barbosa's book.

> The piracies of the Portuguese are told without any reticence, apparently without consciousness of their criminality, for no attempt is made to justify them, and the pretext that such and such an independent state or city did not choose to submit itself on being summoned to do so

by the Portuguese, seems to have been thought all sufficient for laying waste and destroying it. This narrative shows that most of the towns on the coasts of Africa, Arabia, and Persia were in a much more flourishing condition at that time than they have been since the Portuguese ravaged some of them, and interfered with the trade of all.

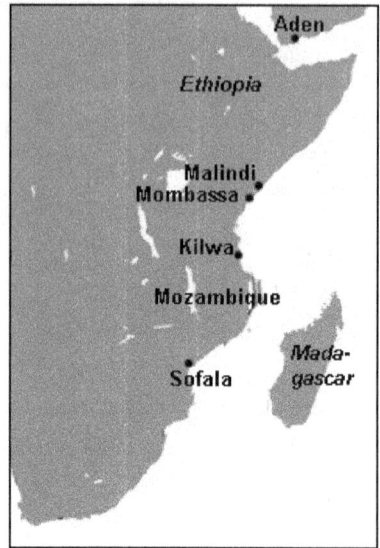

Barbosa does just this: He roams from praising the wealth and beauty of cities to offering cold account of their destruction.

Of Kilwa on the east coast of Africa, Barbosa wrote:

> ... a town of the Moors, built of handsome houses of stone and lime, and very lofty, with their windows like those of the Christians; in the same way it has streets, and these houses have got their terraces, and the wood worked in with the masonry, with plenty of gardens, in which there are many fruit trees and much water. ... the Moors of Sofala, and Zuama, and Anguox, and Mozambique, were all under obedience to the King of Quiloa [Kilwa], who was a great king amongst them. And there is much gold in this town, because all the ships which go to Sofala touch at this island, both in going and coming back.

But ...

> This King, for his great pride, and for not being willing to obey the King of Portugal, had this town taken from him by force, and in it they killed and captured many people, and the King fled from the island, in which the King of Portugal ordered a fortress to be built, and thus he holds under his command and government those who continued to dwell there.

Of Mombasa:

> It is a town of great trade in goods, and has a good port, where there are always many ships, ... This Monbaza is a country well supplied with plenty of provisions, very fine sheep, which have round tails, and many cows, chickens, and very large goats, much rice and millet, and plenty of oranges, sweet and bitter, and lemons, cedrats, pomegranates, Indian figs, and all sorts of vegetables, and very good water.

But ...

> This King, for his pride and unwillingness to obey the King of Portugal, lost his city, and the Portuguese took it from him by force, and the King fled, and they killed and made captives many of his people, and the country was ravaged, and much plunder was carried off from it of gold and silver, copper, ivory, rich stuffs of gold and silk, and much other valuable merchandize.

At Malindi, on the other hand, the Portuguese received a welcome beginning with da Gama's first visit in 1498:

> ... this town has fine houses of stone and whitewash, of several stories, with their windows and terraces, and good streets. ... The trade is great which they carry on in cloth, gold, ivory, copper, quicksilver, and much other merchandise, with both Moors and Gentiles of the kingdom of Cambay ...

And ...

> This King and people have always been very friendly and obedient to the King of Portugal, and the Portuguese have always met with much friendship and good reception amongst them.

Through this sort of sheer brutality the Portuguese disrupted centuries of Indian Ocean trade and established a maritime empire, one held together by outposts with stone forts and by regular visits from Portuguese armadas.

This was the harsh colonial world where Barbosa and Magellan spent their early careers prior to the Armada de Molucca. This was the mindset they carried when they journeyed through the strait and across the Pacific to the Visayans Islands—to Limasawa, then to Cebu, then to Mactan.

The Magellan Expedition

It's not certain when Barbosa came to know Magellan. The two may have met in India, possibly in Cochin in 1512–13 during Magellan's return voyage to Lisbon. By 1518 they were together in Seville, where Barbosa's father, Diogo Barbosa, had settled and become a distinguished Portuguese expatriate. Magellan married Diogo's daughter Beatriz Barbosa Caldera in 1517, shortly after arriving in the city.

Along the voyage Barbosa had a mixed record with Magellan. In Brazil, Barbosa joined crewmates in what became an ongoing orgy with local women. Barbosa went AWOL for three days and nights, prompting Magellan to send a squad of marines to arrest him and clap him in irons. Barbosa got into similar trouble a second time on Cebu, disappearing with local women there.

Mutiny at Puerto San Julián

Barbosa redeemed himself during the mutiny at Puerto San Julián, where Magellan faced a conspiracy among Castilian captains and officers. Among those who remained loyal was Juan Rodríguez Serrano, captain of the *Santiago* and possibly a friend of Barbosa's from his time in India.

With the *Santiago* next to Magellan's flagship *Trinidad*, two carracks were pitted against three that included the powerful San Antonio, the largest of the fleet. Magellan turned the tables with a raid on the *Victoria*, sending Barbosa to lead a boarding party.

Magellan rewarded Barbosa by making him the *Victoria*'s new captain. Barbosa wound up commanding the ship that first circled the globe during that key year in the expedition as it passed through the strait and struggled its way across the Pacific.

More ups and downs followed as the fleet reached East Asia. Magellan demoted Barbosa as captain at Cebu after his second AWOL incident, and then, weeks later, the crew elected Barbosa and Serrano to replace Magellan as co-commanders after their Captain-General's death at Mactan.

Barbosa and Enrique of Malacca

Five days later, their ally on Cebu, Raja Humabon, turned against the Spanish and staged an ambush.

It's unknown who devised the plot, but in his journal, Pigafetta blamed the ambush on Enrique of Malacca, Magellan's slave-interpreter who like Pigafetta was wounded at Mactan. Pigafetta reported:

> As our interpreter, Henrich by name, was wounded slightly, he would not go ashore any more to attend to our necessary affairs, but always kept his bed. On that account, Duarte Barboza, the commander of the flagship, cried out to him and told him, that although his master, the captain, was dead, he was not therefore free; on the contrary he would see to it that when we should reach Espagnia, he should still be the slave of Doña Beatrice, the wife of the captain-general. And threatening the slave that if he did [not] go ashore, he would be flogged ...

Magellan stipulated in his will in 1519 that after his death, Enrique was to be freed. According to Pigafetta, Enrique responded to Barbosa's outburst by going ashore and plotting the attack.

> ... the latter arose, and, feigning to take no heed to those words, went ashore to tell the Christian king [Humabon] that we were about to leave very soon, but that if he would follow his advice, he could gain the ships and all our merchandise. Accordingly they arranged a plot, and the slave returned to the ship, where he showed that he was more cunning than before.

In retrospect, this can be seen only as conjecture, since no investigation could be carried out. More likely Humanbon, disillusioned and in need or protecting his own future, put the plan in action, possibly with Enrique conspiring.

Massacre at Cebu

On May 1, Enrique relayed an invitation from Humabon for the fleet's captains and officers to attend a banquet, where he would give them jewels to carry back to the Christian king. Twenty-six men went ashore, among them Barbosa, Serrano, and other top officers.

At the last minute, two of them, João de Lopes Carvalho and Gonzalo Gómez de Espinosa, grew suspicious and hurried back to the ships. Just as they arrived, the crew heard shouting from beyond the beach. According to Pigafetta, who was wounded and stayed on board:

> Twenty-four men went ashore, among whom was our astrologer, San Martín de Sivilla. I could not go because I was all swollen up by a wound from a poisoned arrow which I had received in my face. Jovan Carvaio and the constable returned, and told us that they saw the man who had been cured by a miracle take the priest to his house. Consequently, they had left that place, because they suspected some evil. Scarcely had they spoken those words when we heard loud cries and lamentations.

> We immediately weighed anchor and discharging many mortars into the houses, drew in nearer to the shore. While thus discharging [our pieces] we saw Juan Serrano in his shirt bound and wounded, crying to us not to fire any more, for the natives would kill him. We asked him whether all the others and the interpreter were dead. He said that they were all dead except the interpreter.

Carvalho, suddenly a senior officer, made the decision to flee before the Spanish ships were attacked. It's unclear from different accounts whether he abandoned Serrano there on the beach or whether Serrano ordered him to escape, though Pigafetta reported the former.

> He begged us earnestly to redeem him with some of the merchandise; but Johan Carvaio, his boon companion, [and others] would not allow the boat to go ashore so that they might remain masters of the ships. But although Juan Serrano weeping asked us not to set sail so quickly, for they would kill him, and said that he prayed God to ask his soul of Johan Carvaio, his comrade, in the day of judgment, we immediately departed. I do not know whether he is dead or alive.

The three ships left immediately, so details of the attack were never learned. Enrique of Malacca was never again seen by the Europeans.

Again, if Magellan's Barbosa was the travel chronicler, his death at Cebu possibly meant a huge loss of historical knowledge. And had Pigafetta not been injured at Mactan, he too would have attended the banquet and been killed, and we would know very little about Magellan's expedition today.

As for Juan Serrano, he was last seen beaten on the beach at Cebu. He may have been killed there, though it's been suggested he was kept alive and sold as a slave, possibly in China.

---

1. Records show Duarte Barbosa was a relation of Ferdinand Magellan's through marriage, likely Magellan's brother-in-law, but possible his wife's cousin.

2. Henry Edward John Stanley, 3rd Baron Stanley of Alderley, (1827–1903) was a historian who translated several works on the Age of Discovery including Barbosa's book and *The First Voyage Round the World by Magellan*, which included the accounts of Antonio Pigafetta and others who made the journey. Stanley became fascinated with the East as a boy and sometime around 1859 converted to Islam, making him the first Muslim member of the House of Lords.

3. This is a good point to stop and remember that history is written not by the victors but by the victors' writers. Had Barbosa survived to write his own account of the expedition, we might have a very different picture of events and of the people involved. (Treat and pay your writers well.)

4. Records show there were three Duarte Barbosas in India at that time. Historians including Stanley and Dames credited Magellan's Barbosa as the author, whereas recent studies point to a different Barbosa. The Magellan biographer Tim Joyner noted that of the three Barbosas, the author had "a propensity for getting into trouble for neglecting his job," at one point causing Alfonso de Albuquerque to clap him in irons. Magellan punished his relation twice for the same behavior.

11.

Magellan's Real Circumnavigation

The man most credited with the first circumnavigation never circled the globe and he never
tried. Few people know Ferdinand Magellan's
true story, that he was killed in the Philippines
halfway through the first circumnavigation in
1519–22, and moreover, that he still came within
2,600 kilometers (1,615 miles) of fully circling
the earth.1

Magellan

Magellan's own circumnavigation began fourteen years earlier. In
1505, Magellan sailed eastward to India (around the Cape of Good
Hope) with Portugal's viceroy Francisco de Almeida. This was a
colonizing fleet sent to exploit Vasco da Gama's "discoveries." It
consisted of 21 ships and 1,500 men, among them nobleman-soldiers
like Magellan, as well as merchants, shoemakers, carpenters, priests,
barbers, judges, and physicians. The fleet has been likened to that of
the Pilgrims; its aim was to set up colonies and stay.

In 1509 Magellan was with the first Portuguese fleet to reach
Southeast Asia, visiting the Malacca Sultanate, a wealthy trade hub
on the Malay Peninsula. Under the command of Diogo Lopes de
Sequeira, the Europeans did not fare well on this debut in the region—
merchants in Malacca knew of Portuguese atrocities in India just as
merchants did in the Philippines and Brunei a decade later.

The Sultan of Malacca initially welcomed the small fleet, but three
days later set up an ambush. He offered the Portuguese a cargo of
pepper if only they would send a work party ashore to pick it up.
Overconfident, Sequeira sent a hundred men in longboats under the
command of Magellan's friend (and possibly cousin) Francisco Serrão.
At the same time sampans began rowing to the Portuguese ships, their
occupants smiling and appearing friendly.

Serrão

As the work detail headed from the long-boats to the warehouse where the pepper was said to be, they were attacked by the Sultan's men and cut off from escape.

Reports said Magellan, on board ship, was one of the first to discover the attack. He was able to warn Sequeira and then personally row a skiff directly into the fray. Diving into the fight, Magellan helped save Serrão and led a number of the other Portuguese back to the ships. The fleet escaped back to Cochin.

A year and a half later, in 1511, Magellan returned as part of a much-larger fleet led by Portugal's Afonzo de Albuquerque, a man known for brutal vengeance. Although far outnumbered by the Sultan's 20,000 men and 3,000 dug-in cannons, the Portuguese crushed the city's defenses, forcing the Sultan to flee. The Portuguese had only about 1,000 assault troops, among them Magellan.

At the height of battle, the Sultan himself led a charge of twenty war elephants against the Europeans, a terrifying sight that sent the invaders running—all but two, who stood their ground and attacked the royal elephant with lances. Hit in the eye and the stomach, the animal roared in pain, upsetting the entire line of elephants, and causing the elephants to bolt, the Sultan fleeing with them.

One reason the Portuguese were able to overcome the odds in manpower was Europeans' attitude toward war. In Southeast Asia, manpower was a key commodity, and humans were a main goal of invasions. Attacking armies tried not to kill unnecessarily. The strategy was more to surprise and terrify, and take the conquered population alive.

The Portuguese, conversely, had no such concerns, and were fully ready to slaughter huge numbers of soldiers and civilians, and many of those in Malacca in 1511 had done just that in Africa and India.

After Malacca fell, the invaders systematically sacked the city, pillaging the homes of wealthy Muslim merchants. Their booty included gold bars, jewels, wonders from China, and slaves—including a teenage boy claimed by Magellan and christened Enrique.

Chinese and Indian merchants who had aided the Portuguese were spared. They were given flags to pin on their buildings to mark them as off-limits.

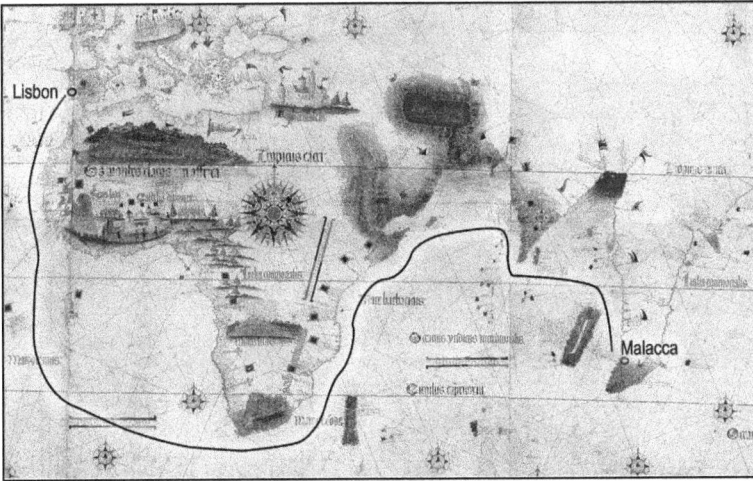

Rough extent of Magellan's early travels.

Not long after, Magellan's friend Serrão sailed with a small fleet and, separated, became the first Portuguese to reach the Moluccas, or Spice Islands. There, he ignored orders to return to Malacca and instead married the daughter of a local sultan. Serrão wrote letters to Magellan describing a tropical paradise rich in spices, and Magellan became fixated on joining his friend.

In a return letter, Magellan wrote: "God willing, I will soon be seeing you, whether by way of Portugal or Castile, for that is how my affairs have been leaning ..." By Castile, he meant sailing for the Spanish crown, instead of the Portuguese king.

Magellan wound up trying to join Francisco Serrão in the Moluccas, but instead of traveling 2,600 kilometers east from Malacca to the Moluccas, Magellan took the long way—a scenic route certainly—westbound around much of the earth.

Combat in Morocco

Magellan returned to Lisbon in 1512 or 1513, bringing with him Enrique, the slave he claimed at Malacca. The Malay teenager was about all the fortune Magellan had to show for seven years' service in India—from where a single shipment of spices returned to Europe could set a person up for life. Magellan invested what he had collected in a trade deal that went sour, a slap in the face he learned of on his return to Lisbon.

Azamor

In August 1513, Magellan was pressed into service in a cavalry unit sent to Morocco. To put down a rebellion in Azamor (Azemmour), southwest of Casablanca, King Manuel I launched a major assault on the coastal city. Magellan joined a gigantic force of 500 ships, 13,000 foot soldiers, and 2,000 cavalry—the largest ever sent from Portugal, a kingdom that suddenly had substantial wealth pouring in from Asia and Africa at its disposal.

This was among Magellan's practical experience leading up to the Magellan-Elcano expedition: serving as a soldier with sometimes huge, far-flung fleets.

At Azamor, Magellan was among the first to land and reach the city walls, and as in the past, his spirit outpaced his luck. His horse was quickly killed by a lance, and shortly after, Magellan himself was hit by one in the knee—sustaining an injury that left him with a permanent limp. It was one of several times Magellan was wounded in battle.

On returning to Lisbon, Magellan had a falling-out with King Manuel I, one that festered over several audiences with Portugal's monarch. In one final meeting, Magellan asked Manuel if he could go elsewhere to offer his services, and the king responded that Magellan could go where he pleased.

Humiliated, Magellan followed through on his threat to reach the Moluccas "by way of Castile" if needed. In 1518, he defected to Spain.

---

1. *Ferdinand Magellan* is the English version of the Portuguese *Fernão de Magalhães*. In Spanish the name is *Fernando de Magallanes*.

* Continued in Chapter 13 (an unlucky number).

12.

Gómez de Espinosa: Master-at-Arms

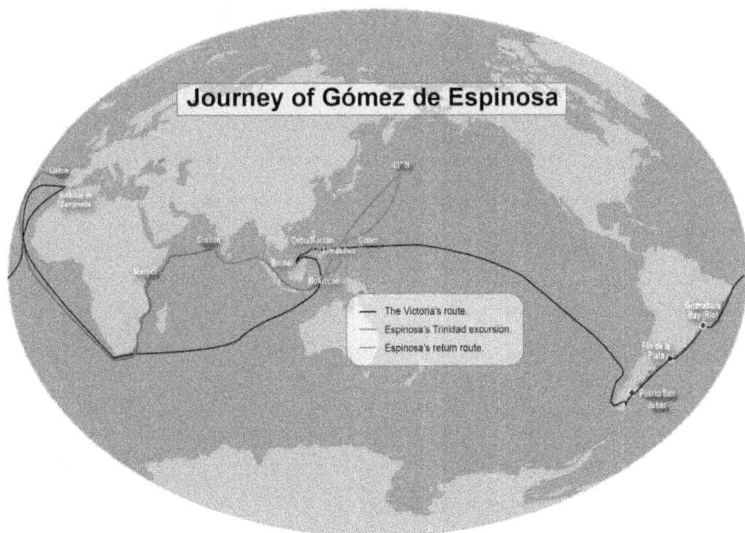

FOR GONZALO GÓMEZ DE ESPINOSA, the first circumnavigation was far longer than it was for the others in the fleet, both in distance and time. Espinosa's circle included side trips from the Spice Islands to North Pacific waters well east of Hokkaido—and back—and later along the coasts of India and East Africa as a Portuguese prisoner. Espinosa did not return to Spain until 1527, four and a half years after Juan Sebastián Elcano led the *Victoria* back and eight years after the fleet departed in 1519.

Gómez de Espinosa played several key roles in the expedition. During the Easter mutiny, Espinosa was at the center of Magellan's offensive to recover the *Victoria* (he stabbed its captain in the throat), and it was Espinosa who led the *Trinidad* back into the Pacific on a cartographic gamble that if successful might have brought Ferdinand Magellan's flagship to Canada or the US West Coast.

Espinosa also journeyed far in rank, going from master-at-arms (basically a shipboard police officer) to captain general of the fleet and captain of the *Trinidad*.

The Atlantic and Brazil

What Espinosa had to offer was loyalty, to his duty and to Magellan. From the start Magellan was facing a conspiracy among his Castilian officers, and he built a close relationship with Espinosa knowing he was going to need some law enforcement on his side.

That conspiracy became a problem early on. During the Atlantic crossing Magellan personally arrested Juan de Cartagena for insubordination, causing the Castilian officer to openly call for mutiny. Cartagena was captain of the *San Antonio*, the armada's largest ship, and inspector general of the fleet—an assignment made by Spanish officials as a check on Magellan's power. Cartagena wound up briefly in chains and for the next six months in custody.

Once across the Atlantic Ocean, the fleet stopped over in Brazil, a visit that quickly degenerated into an orgy with the local women, both onshore and aboard ship. After several days, Magellan gave Espinosa the unpopular task of rounding up the crew onshore and clearing the ships of women, so the fleet could prepare to depart. Among those on shore was Duarte Barbosa, AWOL for three days. Magellan sent a squad of marines to bring him back.

The Easter Mutiny

Espinosa was central in Magellan's response to the mutiny at Puerto San Julián. The mutineers took control of three ships, the *San Antonio*, the *Concepción*, and the *Victoria*. On the *San Antonio*, they killed its master, Juan de Elorriaga, and put its captain, Álvaro de Mesquita, in chains.

With three ships including the large *San Antinio*, the mutineers had a serious advantage. Briefly it appeared that Magellan was finished, but the Castilians overlooked or underestimated their captain-general's military background in campaigns in Africa, India, and Malacca.

Magellan focused first on the *Victoria*. He sent Espinosa to hand-deliver a message to the *Victoria*'s Captain, Luis Mendoza. With a marine escort and two sailors rowing, their skiff came alongside the *Victoria*, where Mendoza refused to let them board. Espinosa taunted the *Victoria*'s captain, asking if he were afraid of an unarmed man.

Pride wounded, Mendoza let Espinosa and his escort climb aboard and led the two to his cabin to read Magellan's message. Mendoza was wearing armor but no helmet. After reading Magellan's message, he let out a defiant laugh and thrust it back.

Struggle aboard the *Victoria*.

Espinosa responded by thrusting a hidden dagger into Mendoza's throat; the marine followed with a dagger blow to the skull, killing Mendoza instantly.

Meanwhile, Barbosa had led a boarding party of fifteen men, unseen, to the *Victoria* and on a signal from Espinosa they climbed aboard and disarmed the crew on deck. The rest of the men offered no further resistance—of the three ships that mutinied, the *Victoria* had the most Portuguese and non-Castilian crew members. Magellan likely chose his target with that in mind.

With three ships now on Magellan's side, guarding the harbor's entrance, the *Trinidad* noticed activity aboard the *San Antonio*. Her gun ports were opened and her bow pointed seaward; it looked as if an explosive escape was planned. Exactly what happened is uncertain. The next morning, an anchor either failed or was cut, and the *San Antonio* was left drifting helplessly toward the *Trinidad*.

As it approached, Quesada was seen in full armor carrying a lance and shield, barking orders that his crew completely ignored. The *Trinidad* fired a few shots at the *San Antonio*'s hull before a boarding party jumped over and rounded up the mutineers. After that, the *Concepción* quickly surrendered as well.

Barbosa had redeemed himself after going AWOL in Brazil. Magellan rewarded his relation by making him the new captain of the *Victoria*. Espinosa eventually became captain of the *Trinidad*.[1]

-----

1. Read more in Chapter 14.

13.

Magellan and the Battle of Mactan

Magellan's and Enrique's Second World Tour

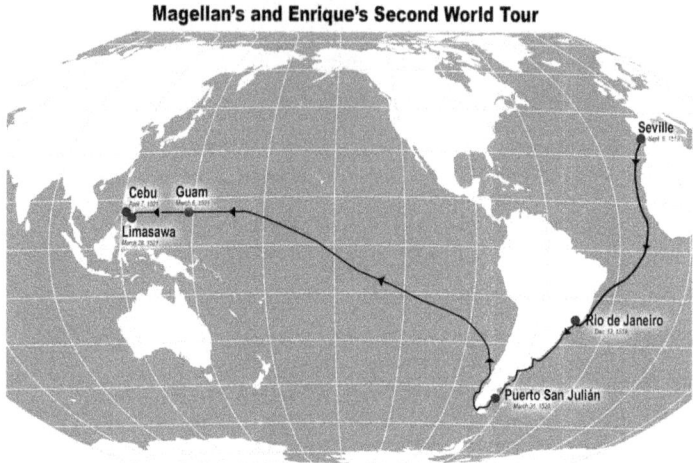

PEOPLE DEBATE the labels: *explorer, navigator, adventurer, discoverer* and of course from the opposite perspective, *colonizer*. A better term for Magellan and Columbus is *explorer-conqueror*. The same goes for Henry the Navigator, Vasco da Gama, and later the likes of James Cook. They were out not just to find but to keep.

As the historian Yuval Harari wrote in his book *Sapiens*: "... early modern Europeans caught a fever that drove them to sail to distant and completely unknown lands full of alien cultures, take one step on to their beaches, and immediately declare, 'I claim all these territories for my king!'"

Magellan succeeded at the explorer part of his job: He found a strait that led to Balboa's South Sea, managed to cross the unexpectedly large "sea," and named things along the way including the Pacific Ocean itself. And when the fleet arrived at Limasawa, Magellan proved the world was round.

But soon after, Magellan got started on the conquering part of the job title, and that didn't go so well.

At Cebu Magellan made an alliance with a local ruler, Raja Humabon, whom he baptized along with hundreds of others as

Christians. (Religion has been used often in history to subjugate populations—and control trade—including in Southeast Asia before the arrival of Europeans.)

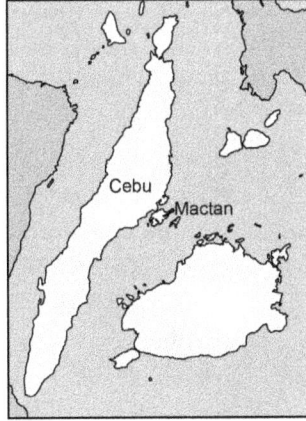

Magellan sided with Humabon against Lapulapu, the datu of the neighboring island of Mactan.[1] Siding with one state against another was a strategy the Portuguese learned in India. For Magellan, though, the alliance would be a fatal one.

When Lapulapu refused to pay a tribute to Humabon as Magellan had ordered, Magellan again turned to the Portuguese tactics of Vasco da Gama and Francisco de Almeida in East Africa and India—he responded immediately with force.

Magellan boasted to Humabon that a single armored soldier of his could take on a hundred of the raja's warriors, and he put on fighting demonstrations to prove the assertion. Looking back on seven years' experience in Asia and on his Morocco campaign, Magellan reckoned a small force from his fleet could quickly beat a small island village into submission.

Battle of Mactan

At daybreak on April 27, 1521, Magellan led a force of just 60 well-armed volunteers in three shallops from Cebu to Mactan. Leaving boat crews behind, he and 48 men waded (waddled?) ashore to attack.

There is more than one account of the events that day. Here is the most detailed (and colorful) version, written by Antonio Pigafetta, chronicler of the Magellan-Elcano expedition.

> The musketeers and crossbowmen shot from a distance for about a half-hour, but uselessly; for the shots only passed through the shields which were made of thin wood and the arms ... When our muskets were discharged, the natives would never stand still, but leaped hither and thither, covering themselves ... They shot so many arrows at us and hurled so many bamboo spears (some of them tipped with iron) at the captain-general, besides pointed stakes hardened with fire, stones, and mud, that we could scarcely defend ourselves ...

So many of them charged down upon us that they shot the captain through the right leg with a poisoned arrow. On that account, he ordered us to retire slowly, but the men took to flight, except six or eight of us who remained with the captain. The natives shot only at our legs, for the latter were bare; and so many were the spears and stones that they hurled at us, that we could offer no resistance.

The mortars in the boats could not aid us as they were too far away. So we continued to retire for more than a

Mactan.

good crossbow flight from the shore always fighting up to our knees in the water. The natives continued to pursue us, and picking up the same spear four or six times, hurled it at us again and again.

Recognizing the captain, so many turned upon him that they knocked his helmet off his head twice, but he always stood firmly like a good knight, together with some others. Thus did we fight for more than one hour, refusing to retire farther. An Indian hurled a bamboo spear into the captain's face, but the latter immediately killed him with his lance, which he left in the Indian's body.

Then, trying to lay hand on sword, he could draw it out but halfway, because he had been wounded in the arm with a bamboo spear. When the natives saw that, they all hurled themselves upon him. One of them wounded him on the left leg with a large cutlass, which resembles a scimitar, only being larger. That caused the captain to fall face downward, when immediately they rushed upon him with iron and bamboo spears and with their cutlasses, until they killed our mirror, our light, our comfort, and our true guide.

When they wounded him, he turned back many times to see whether we were all in the boats. Thereupon, beholding him dead, we, wounded, retreated, as best we could, to the boats, which were already pulling off.

Among those last to retreat were Pigafetta and Magellan's slave-interpreter Enrique of Malacca, both wounded in the fight. Also killed in the battle was Cristóbal Rabelo, possibly an illegitimate son of Magellan's.

Pigafetta went on with final praise for Magellan.

> Had it not been for that unfortunate captain, not a single one of us would have been saved in the boats, for while he was fighting the others retired to the boats.

> I hope through [the efforts of] your most illustrious Lordship that the fame of so noble a captain will not become effaced in our times. Among the other virtues which he possessed, he was more constant than ever any one else in the greatest of adversity. He endured hunger better than all the others, and more accurately than any man in the world did he understand sea charts and navigation. And that this was the truth was seen openly, for no other had had so much natural talent nor the boldness to learn how to circumnavigate the world, as he had almost done.

While Magellan did reach Asia, he never made it to the Moluccas, his destination, and reunite with his friend Francisco Serrão. In fact, Serrão was killed around the same time—on the same day according to one account—likely a poisoning.

It would be six months before two of the remaining ships reached the Spice Islands, where the notion of circling the globe was finally considered, and a year and a half before the *Victoria* returned to Seville. But as a result of Pigafetta's praise and efforts, it is Ferdinand Magellan who people today most associate with the first circumnavigation.

---

1. The first Filipino leader to fight Spanish colonialism, Lapulapu has become a national hero in the Philippines. As a result his story has taken on a political flavor, right down to the spelling of his name. In December 2021, then-president Rodrigo Duterte issued an executive order requiring the private and public sectors to spell the name closed as one word (*Lapulapu*), and not hyphenated (*Lapu-Lapu*). The following month, Duterte made news again by proclaiming he was unhappy that the statue of Ferdinand Magellan on Cebu was taller than one of Lapulapu on the island, saying the Mactan datu's statue should have been higher. In history, size matters.

14.

Espinosa: Unlikely Captain-General

MOST OF THE FLEET'S remaining pilots and officers were killed in the massacre on Cebu on May 1, 1521, among them Duarte Barbosa and Juan Serrano, the two captains chosen to replace Magellan. The crew was so small, they could no longer maintain the three remaining ships. They scuttled the *Concepción* off the coast of a nearby island and sailed on.

Gonzalo Gómez de Espinosa and João de Lopes Carvalho were elected to be the fleet's new commanders, Espinosa as captain of the *Victoria* and Carvalho as captain of the *Trinidad* and captain general of the fleet. For Espinosa it was a jump in rank from the equivalent of a modern marine warrant officer to ship's captain. A year after supporting Magellan in the mutiny at Puerto San Julián, Espinosa had been rewarded.

Four months later on September 21, Carvalho was deposed as captain general and Espinosa was elected to replace him. Espinosa, now the fleet's ranking officer, took the helm of the *Trinidad*, while the *Concepción*'s original master, Juan Sebastián Elcano, became captain of the *Victoria*.

With only two of the fleet's five ships remaining, they pushed on, finally reaching Tidore in the Moluccas on November 8. Magellan's fleet (or part of it) had arrived at its destination, the Spice Islands, after more than two years.

By mid-December the two ships were loaded with spices and ready to return home. On departure, however, the *Trinidad*'s hull was severely damaged. The ship would have to be emptied and repaired, which would take time.

Two threats were looming: One, they learned the Portuguese were headed their way, which would mean certain capture, and two, the monsoon winds were about to shift; if they didn't leave immediately, sailing northwest or west would be impossible for the season.

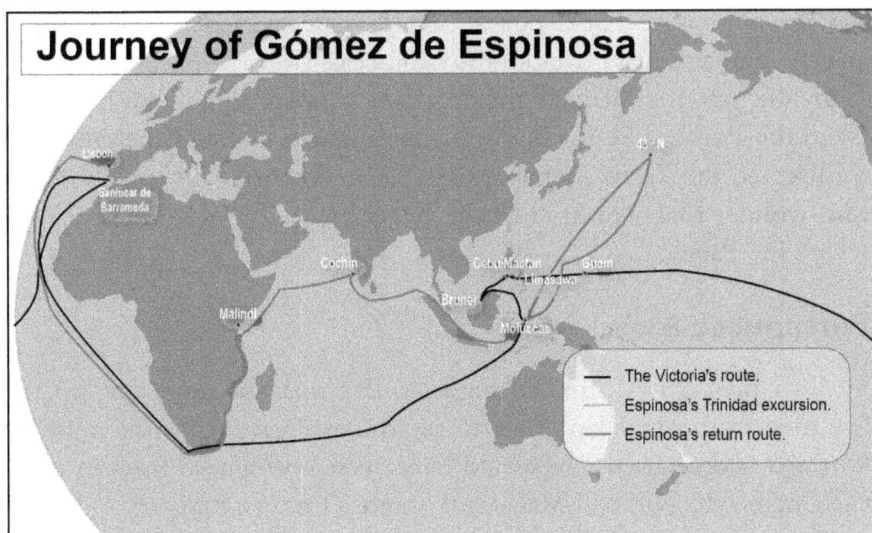

Journey of Gómez de Espinosa

— The Victoria's route.
— Espinosa's Trinidad excursion.
— Espinosa's return route.

Thus they made the decision for the *Victoria* to leave first, ahead of the shift in winds. Captained by Elcano, the *Victoria* departed on December 21, 1521, and after passing Timor headed straight across the Indian Ocean through uncharted waters, avoiding the traditional trade routes along the Indian and East African coasts, which were controlled by the Portuguese.

Hokkaido

Hokkaido is not a location that normally comes to mind when talking about Ferdinand Magellan's expedition, but Espinosa led the *Trinidad* deep into the North Pacific well to the east of Japan's northernmost island.

Back in the Moluccas, it took four months to repair the *Trinidad*'s hull. Espinosa finally departed on April 6 with the plan of returning eastward across the Pacific. But instead of retracing the fleet's original crossing from the south, they headed northward, hoping to catch westerly winds like those in the North Atlantic.

As the *Trinidad* sailed well east of southern Japan, the crew began to run out of provisions and were left with only rice to eat. Cold temperatures and scurvy began to take a toll on the crew, as well. The *Trinidad* sailed to a point in the North Pacific roughly 43° N and 165° E of Greenwich where it was hit by a heavy storm. The resulting damage was severe enough that Espinosa and his officers made the decision to turn around and head back to the Moluccas.

By the time they arrived, the crew was so weak and ill that Espinosa asked the Portuguese for help. The Portuguese arrested the crew and confiscated the *Trinidad*'s papers, books, and charts—it was no doubt with wonder that they studied the fleet's route through the strait and across the Pacific.

Portuguese Asia

As a prisoner of the Portuguese, Espinosa became one of the few men from Magellan's fleet to see the extensive maritime network Portugal had secured. He would have seen Portuguese forts in cities like Cochin (Kochi) and Malacca. Espinosa's return itinerary took him to Ternate, Banda, Java, Malacca, Cochin, and Lisbon, a route that toured both coasts of Africa.

After returning to Spain in 1527, Espinosa became one of several survivors of Magellan's expedition who had to fight for money owed to them or their families. In 1529, Charles V finally awarded Espinosa with a life pension that he would live comfortably on.

As late as 1543, Gonzalo Gómez de Espinosa was still alive and well in Seville, at the age of 60, likely telling tall tales that required little exaggeration to thrill listeners.

15.

Juan Sebastián Elcano
Circles the Globe

Juan Sebastián Elcano

JUAN SEBASTIÁN ELCANO has received much of the glory for the first circumnavigation—it was Elcano who led the *Victoria* from Tidore in the Spice Islands back to Seville in 1522.

Elcano entered the fleet with a legal cloud over his head, and he played a major role in the mutiny at Puerto San Julián, earning himself a death sentence. But he was in an unlikely place at an unlikely time.

Elcano was a professional mariner of Basque origin. Before joining Magellan's fleet, he became the master of a ship chartered by the crown of Castile, trading along the coast of North Africa. At one point, to pay his crew he took a short-term loan and was afterward forced to repay the sum by selling the ship—a violation of Castilian law, selling crown property to foreigners.

Elcano entered Magellan's armada originally as master's mate, then master, aboard the *Concepción*. He fell in with the *Concepción*'s captain and other Castilian officers opposed to Magellan. During the Easter mutiny, the *San Antonio*'s master was killed, and Elcano was brought aboard to prepare the ship, the fleet's largest, for an attack on Magellan's flagship.

After the mutiny was put down, Elcano was one of forty men sentenced to death, though Magellan could ill afford to lose that many men, especially skilled mariners. As with most of the forty, Elcano's sentence was reduced.

After the *Concepción* was scuttled near Cebu, Elcano moved to the *Victoria* as master, and then on September 21, 1521, became captain of the ship. Later at Tidore, the decision was made to continue westward to return to Spain and thus complete the first circumnavigation. It was fear of the Portuguese that prompted the route—by no means the original plan.

Elcano and the *Victoria* departed Tidore on December 21, 1521. It was five months later, on May 22 that the ship passed the Cape of Good Hope and entered the Atlantic. It took another four months to reach Sanlúcar de Barrameda, on the coast just south of Seville.

In October 1522 Elcano was honored by Charles V at Valladolid and given a large annual pension and assigned a royal commission. But life on shore didn't agree with Juan Sebastián Elcano. He had children with two different women and was for some reason receiving death threats, possibly from survivors of the expedition.

In July 1525, Elcano sailed again with a seven-ship fleet that set out to retrace Magellan's route. South of Patagonia, Elcano was at first unable to locate the strait, and just as he did, the fleet was hit by a storm that sent Elcano's ship onto a beach. Most the crew were saved and Elcano transferred to a different ship, the *Santa Maria de Victoria*.

The expedition went downhill from there. Two ships deserted while sailing the strait, and in the Pacific the fleet was separated during a storm. The *Santa Maria de Victoria* found itself crossing the Pacific alone and soon suffering the same problem Magellan's fleet had— scurvy, a condition brought on by lack of vitamin C. In July as they crossed the equator, Elcano made a will. Four days later, the ship's captain succumbed, leaving Elcano in command. A week later, Juan Sebastián Elcano himself died.

In 1872, Spain's King Phillip II granted Elcano's heirs with rule over the Marquisate of Buglas, on Negros Island in the Philippines. The surname Elcano is the most common in the Philippines today.

16.

Jules Verne, Pigafetta, and That Pesky International Date Line

B OTH PHILEAS FOGG in *Around the World in Eighty Days* and the survivors of the Magellan-Elcano expedition circumnavigated the globe, the former eastward in the 1870s, the latter westward in the 1520s. Both Fogg and Elcano's crew were surprised to have gained (Fogg) or lost (Elcano) a day, and both Jules Verne in his 1873 classic novel and Antonio Pigafetta, the Magellan-Elcano chronicler, tell a similar story of their surprise discovery.

Phileas Fogg

One of the most famous circumnavigations was Phileas Fogg's in *Around the World in Eighty Days*, Jules Verne's 1873 novel. In it (spoiler alert[1]), Phileas Fogg is nearly ruined financially when he is unexpectedly saved, discovering he gained a day while traveling.

Jules Verne, 1873:

Passepartout went on his errand enchanted. He soon reached the clergyman's house, but found him not at home. Passepartout waited a good twenty minutes, and when he left the reverend gentleman, it was thirty-five minutes past eight. But in what a state he was! With his hair in disorder, and without his hat, he ran along the street as never man was seen to run before, overturning passers-by, rushing over the sidewalk like a waterspout.

In three minutes he was in Saville Row again, and staggered back into Mr. Fogg's room.

He could not speak.

"What is the matter?" asked Mr. Fogg.

"My master!" gasped Passepartout—"marriage—impossible—"

"Impossible?"

"Impossible—for to-morrow."

"Why so?"

"Because to-morrow—is Sunday!"

"Monday," replied Mr. Fogg.

"No—to-day is Saturday."

"Saturday? Impossible!"

"Yes, yes, yes, yes!" cried Passepartout. "You have made a mistake of one day! We arrived twenty-four hours ahead of time; but there are only ten minutes left!"

Passepartout had seized his master by the collar, and was dragging him along with irresistible force.

Phileas Fogg, thus kidnapped, without having time to think, left his house, jumped into a cab, promised a hundred pounds to the cabman, and, having run over two dogs and overturned five carriages, reached the Reform Club.

The clock indicated a quarter before nine when he appeared in the great saloon.

Phileas Fogg had accomplished the journey round the world in eighty days! . . .

How was it that a man so exact and fastidious could have made this error of a day? How came he to think that he had arrived in London on Saturday, the twenty-first day of December, when it was really Friday, the twentieth, the seventy-ninth day only from his departure?

The cause of the error is very simple.

Phileas Fogg had, without suspecting it, gained one day on his journey, and this merely because he had travelled constantly eastward; he would, on the contrary, have lost a day had he gone in the opposite direction, that is, westward.

In journeying eastward he had gone towards the sun, and the days therefore diminished for him as many times four minutes as he crossed degrees in this direction. There are three hundred and sixty degrees on the circumference of the earth; and these three hundred and sixty degrees, multiplied by four minutes, gives precisely twenty-four hours— that is, the day unconsciously gained. In other words, while Phileas Fogg, going eastward, saw the sun pass the meridian eighty times, his friends in London only saw it pass the meridian seventy-nine times. This is why they awaited him at the Reform Club on Saturday, and not Sunday, as Mr. Fogg thought.

Phileas Fogg's circumnavigation began and ended at his London apartment on Saville Row. The Magellan-Elcano expedition began and ended in the Spanish city of Seville.

Antonio Pigafetta, 350 years earlier:

Had not God given us good weather we would all have perished of hunger. Finally, constrained by our great extremity, we went to the islands of Capo Verde.

Wednesday, July nine, we reached one of those islands called Sancto Jacobo [Santiago], and immediately sent the boat ashore for food, with the story for the Portuguese that we had lost our foremast under the equinoctial line (although we had lost it upon the cape of Bonna Speranza), and when we were restepping it, our captain-general had gone to Spagnia with the other two ships.

With those good words and with our merchandise, we got two boatloads of rice. We charged our men when they went ashore in the boat to ask what day it was, and they told us that it was Thursday with the Portuguese.

We were greatly surprised for it was Wednesday with us, and we could not see how we had made a mistake; for as I had always kept well, I had set down every day without any interruption.

However, as was told us later, it was no error, but as the voyage had been made continually toward the west and we had returned to the same place as does the sun, we had made that gain of twenty-four hours, as is clearly seen.

Before judging either Pigafetta or Phileas Fogg, stop to remember that even experienced world travelers today get confused and make mistakes because of the loss or gain of a day, a difference further confused on itineraries where departure times are in one time zone and arrival times in another, and red-eye flights often take off after midnight.

---

1. A hundred and fifty years after it was published, Jules Verne's *Around the World in Eight Days* is still a delightful read tucked into a carry-on or downloaded onto your phone while traveling. The book is available for free in multiple formats (Kindle, EPUB, HTML) on the web including at Project Gutenberg (Gutenberg.org).

Additional notes: In his 1890 biography *The Life of Ferdinand Magellan*, F. H. H. Guillemard makes this comment on the international date line: "To the first circumnavigators the necessity of altering their day on passing the meridian of 1 80° was unknown, and so it came about that—the error persisting until quite recent times—Hong-kong and Manila called the same day Monday and Sunday, and it was not until the 31st December, 1844, that the matter was rectified by the omission of that day from the Manilan calendar."

17.

The Circumnavigation of Sir John Mandeville

Left: Mandeville; right: travelers approach
the town dock at Jaffa.

A HANDFUL OF MEDIEVAL TRAVELOGUES were the closest thing Ferdinand Magellan had to a travel guide when he sought a westward route to Asia—accounts credited to Marco Polo, John Mandeville, and others, and those all echoed the same monsters and myths repeated since the time of Pliny the Elder, the Roman author whose *Naturalis Historiae* helped inspire the encyclopedia.

It gets little mention today, but *The Travels of Sir John Mandeville* was a world atlas in medieval Europe, essential reading for navigators and explorers. The accounts became circulated widely in Europe in the fourteenth century. They detail travels in North Africa and the Middle East, and in India, China, and even the Malay Peninsula—which would have been of particular interest to Magellan, and also Enrique of Malacca, Magellan's slave-interpreter.

It was clear early on that much of the Mandeville travelogue was borrowed, yet it's a collection of knowledge and tales and, importantly, a record of the medieval European mindset.

The author introduces himself as Sir John Mandeville, an English knight, though no historical collaboration exists. The work was possibly written by a Flemish monk named Jan de Langhe in the early 1300s, a prolific writer and collector of travelogues. The earliest surviving text is in French.

The departure of Odoric.

It's possible also that the author did not in fact travel: Much of the manuscript is commandeered from other sources. Its accounts of East Asia including the Malay Peninsula mirror those from Odoric of Pordenone (1286–1331), an Italian missionary explorer. A Franciscan friar, Odoric was sent to Asia as a missionary around 1318, and he remained there until 1329. His travels took him well beyond the normal reach of medieval Europeans, to the north coast of Sumatra and the southern coast of China. He may have even reached Lhasa, in Tibet.

One gem among Mandeville's wild tales predicted what would take place two centuries later:

> And therefore hath it befallen many times of one thing that I have heard counted when I was young, how a worthy man departed some-time from our countries for to go search the world. And so he passed India and the isles beyond India, where be more than 5000 isles.
>
> And so long he went by sea and land, and so environed the world by many seasons, that he found an isle where he heard speak his own language, calling on oxen in the plough, such words as men speak to beasts in his own country whereof he had great marvel, for he knew not how it might be.
>
> But I say, that he had gone so long by land and by sea, that he had environed all the earth …

Two hundred years after Mandeville wrote this, it happened. Ferdinand Magellan's slave-interpreter Enrique of Malacca did just what Mandeville's tall tale told. (Read on.)

18.

A World Already Mapped

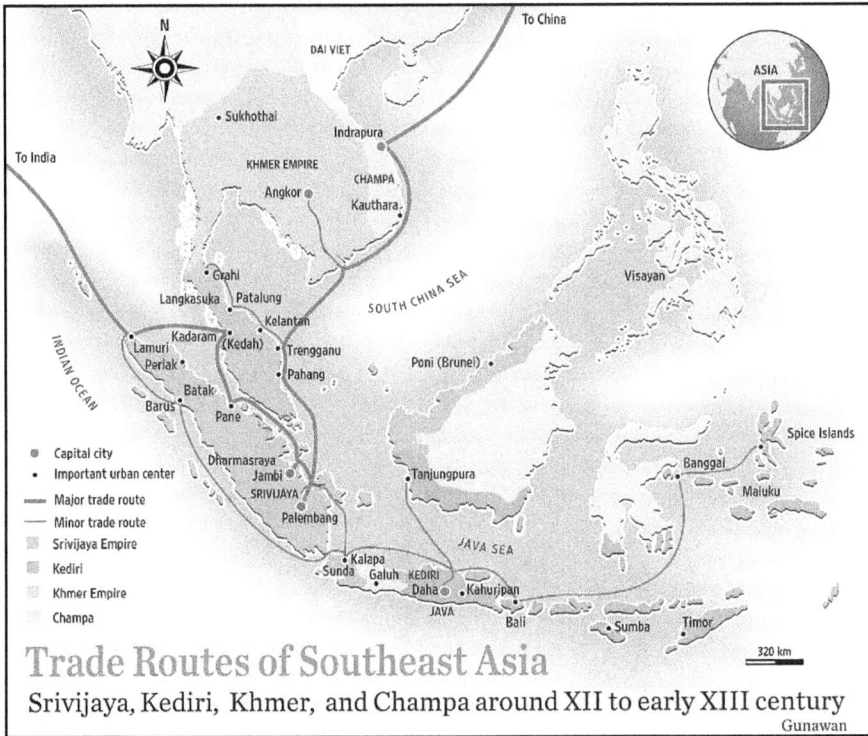

Trade Routes of Southeast Asia
Srivijaya, Kediri, Khmer, and Champa around XII to early XIII century

Gunawan

B Y 2000 BCE, 3,500 years before the medieval Iberians suddenly took an interest in sailing, ancestors of the Austronesian peoples were building and sailing sturdy watercraft that opened up the seas. In search of less-populated lands, they began using outrigger canoes, catamarans, and primitive sails to spread southward from Taiwan to the islands of the Philippines and Indonesia.

Around 700 CE a new surge of expansion took place, and by 1000 CE, Austronesians' seafaring technology had carried people, domesticated animals, and plants to an eastern extreme across the Pacific to Hawaii and the Easter Islands—and possibly to the Americas.

To the west, Austronesian expansion had already reached Madagascar off the coast of Africa.

A world-changing development came in the first millennium BCE when Malay sailors learned to ride the monsoon winds, seasonal

Illustrations of Borobudur Ships.

wind patterns that allowed humans in ships to cross large spans of the Indian Ocean during the correct time of year. Malay sailors were soon supplying the Mediterranean market with cinnamon produced in southern China, and other goods quickly followed. Maritime trade was moving goods from East to West just as the Silk Road was.

In Southeast Asia, two large maritime empires unified peoples and islands over the centuries. The Srivijaya Empire, based on the island of Sumatra, led the expansion of Buddhism across the region from the seventh to the twelfth centuries. As was the case along the Silk Road, religion, ideas, and technology were imported from place to place right alongside silk, spices, and other goods.

Power next moved to the nearby island of Java and the Buddhist-Hindu Majapahit Empire, from the late thirteenth to the early sixteenth centuries.

Majapahit tributaries included modern-day Indonesia, Singapore, Malaysia, southern Thailand, Timor, and the southwestern Philippines. Bas-relief carvings at the Borobudur temple on Java, built around 780, give us a brief look into the lives of eighth-century Javanese, including the ships used in regional trade in the period.

Around the time Majapahit power was fading, China sailed briefly into the picture. The admiral Zheng He[1] (鄭和) led seven grand voyages around Asia and East Africa in the early decades of the fifteenth century, imposing a degree of control over Indian Ocean trade. His fleets dwarfed anything the Europeans would later send. Zheng He's fleets consisted of hundreds of ships carrying as many as 28,000 crew. His flagship famously sported nine masts.

Zheng He's treasure fleets visited Siam, Malacca, Java, Sumatra, India, Arabia, and Africa, impressing, establishing relations, and trading along the way.

Three decades later, Ming China turned inward again and withdrew from the world as suddenly as it had entered. But Zheng He's voyages reshaped Asia's maritime history for the century to come—until the arrival of the Portuguese.

---

1. Zheng He in Wade–Giles: *Chêng-ho.*

19.

Enrique of Malacca, First Circumnavigator

ON MARCH 28, 1521, Enrique of Malacca became the first person to complete a *linguistic* circumnavigation of the globe—he traveled so far in one direction that he reached a point where his language was spoken.

Enrique's journey began a decade earlier following the sack of Malacca, when he was taken as a slave by Ferdinand Magellan. A teenager, he accompanied Magellan back to Portugal, then to Spain, and finally on the

Enrique[1]

Armada de Molucca to locate a westward route to the Spice Islands.

Malacca

When the Chinese admiral Zheng He visited Malacca, he recognized its strategic position on the strait where traffic between East Asia and the Indian Ocean had to pass. He established relations with the city's ruler, Paramesvara, to protect Malacca against attacks from Siam or the Majapahit. He also broke up a nest of Chinese pirates that had formed near Palembang, down the coast of Sumatra. Chinese support gave Malacca time to get established and hold its own.

When the Portuguese arrived a century later in 1509, Malacca was an ultrawealthy city state with a population of over 120,000 people. It was the most cosmopolitan city in the world. Tomé Pires, a Portuguese merchant, counted eighty-four languages spoken in the city. Even the parrots, it was said, were multilingual.

Traders and merchants came from Cairo, Ormuz, Goa, Timor, and Ceylon, as well as China, Cambodia, Java, and Brunei. Peoples became known for the goods they traded: the Gujaratis, Tamils, and Bengalis for cloth; the Chinese for silk, camphor, and porcelain; and

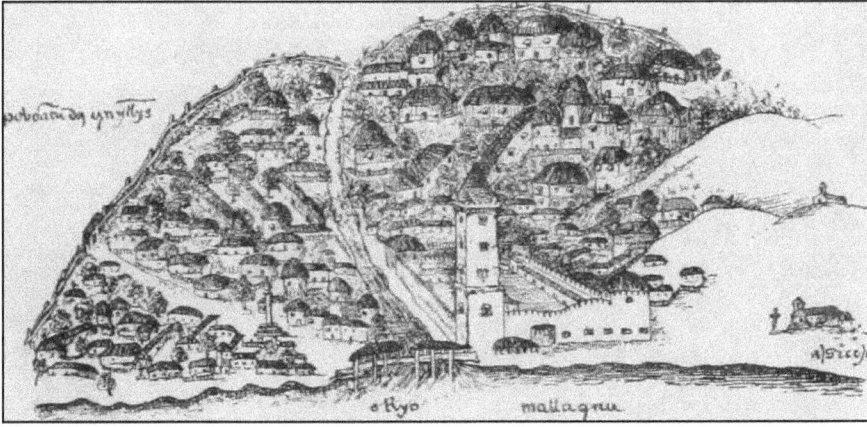

Malacca, drawn by Gaspar Correia in his *Lendas da Índia*, written in the 16th century.

the Malays and other Southeast Asians for spices. Malacca's sizable Chinese population had their own quarter on one side of town, Bukit China ("Chinese Hill").

Pires:

> Malacca is a city made for merchandise, fitter than any other in the world; the end of the monsoons and the beginning of others. Malacca is surrounded and lies in the middle, and the trade and commerce between different nations for a thousand leagues on every hand must come.

At the time Pires was writing this in 1513, Malacca's fortunes were waning. The Portuguese wanted the city to survive as a trade hub, but news of their invasion followed stories of attacks elsewhere, and many merchants took Malacca off their itineraries.

Enrique's First Journey

While in Malacca, Magellan put Enrique to work as an interpreter as he grilled pilots and merchants for knowledge of Asian trade and trade routes. Enrique likely had a talent for languages; numerous Malay dialects were spoken among merchants, and Enrique learned Portuguese and later mastered Spanish.

In 1512 or 1513, Magellan and Enrique made the long voyage to Lisbon, likely stopping at Cochin, Portugal's main stronghold on the Indian coast, and other spots such as Malindi (beach and supplies) on the Kenyan coast along the way.

Enrique of Malacca's Circumnavigation

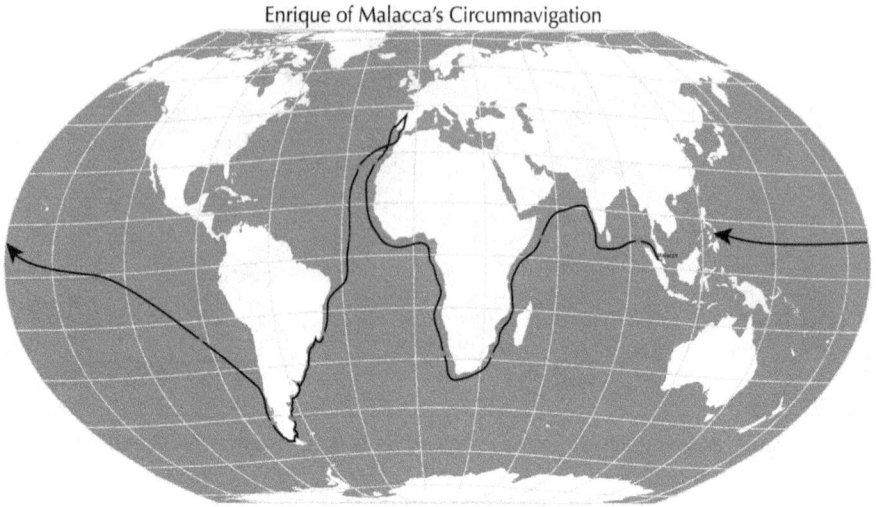

It's unknown how the name Enrique—*Henrique* in Portuguese—was chosen. But the romantic guess says Magellan christened him after Prince Henry (Henrique) the Navigator (actually mostly an armchair navigator), the monarch who began Portugal's drive to sea.[2]

On departure Enrique was forced to learn a lot and learn quickly, beyond just language. That included shipboard routine, possibly climbing masts and handling sails. He had to get accustomed to the clothes worn on board and the sparse foods available at sea. He had to find meals and spots on or below deck to sleep. They had at best roll-up straw mattresses, and at times were lucky to find somewhere dry to lay those mattresses out. Then there were ever-present smells, the stench of bilgewater and livestock, those as a backdrop to pitching and rocking on the waves.

And while surrounded by water in every direction for months, Enrique likely *missed* water—freshwater, that is, for drinking and bathing in. Europeans considered bathing unnecessarily dangerous, while Southeast Asians considered it essential for purification and cooling. At sea bathing was rare and usually only saltwater was available.

And whereas the Chinese drank tea and the Europeans wine, the common drink in Southeast Asia was water. Among ships' supplies, the most important provision was not water but wine.

One can picture Enrique arriving in Lisbon to find further disappointment in Iberian cuisine on land. Throughout Southeast Asia, meat was a small part in the diet and was usually eaten fresh, shortly after slaughter. For Europeans, conversely, meat was a constant staple, often salted or covered with spices to hide its rotting taste.

The Armada de Molucca

Enrique and Magellan probably arrived in Lisbon in 1513, meaning Enrique spent close to six years in Europe. In September 1519 as they prepared to sail on Magellan's great enterprise, Enrique was one of the more-experienced crew members on board, and also one of the more-highly paid.

Enrique was enlisted as an interpreter with a monthly salary of 1,500 maravedis. That's the same amount that Magellan's brother-in-law, Duarte Barbosa, was earning and 300 more per month than Cristovão Rebêlo, who was possibly Magellan's illegitimate son.

By comparison, Franciso Albo was signed as master's mate on the *Trinidad* at 2,000 maravedis while Juan Sebastián Elcano was signed as master on the *Concepción* at 3,000 maravedis.

Of course, when valuing Enrique's work skills, no one knew the fleet would have to travel for a year and a half before the young man could do any interpreting.

Enrique's Circumnavigation

A Disney film about Enrique of Malacca would certainly center on the fleet's arrival at Limasawa Island as a triumphant climax. The armada had just spent three harrowing months at sea, losing thirty crew members to scurvy and starvation, and at the third or fourth island they called on, they were met by eight men in a canoe. Presumably to everyone's surprise and delight, Enrique could converse with them, likely using a Malay dialect common in regional trade.

Enrique had circumnavigated the globe *linguistically*, and Magellan had just produced empirical proof that the world was round. Both Enrique and Magellan had come about 2,600 kilometers (1,615 miles) from a full circle of the earth, Malacca being the starting point.

Enrique may well have gone on. After the massacre at Cebu, Enrique basically defected from the Spanish fleet and from history in

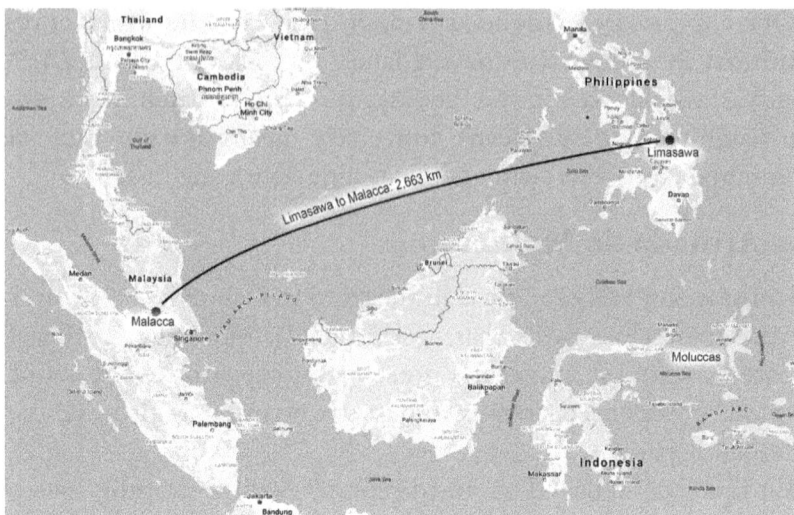

the process. But journeying on was possible. Limasawa and neighboring islands were part of a trade network that dealt in gold and slaves as well as spices, and was extensive enough that merchants there knew of Portuguese atrocities at Malacca, Calicut, and greater India.

Finding passage from Limasawa to Sumatra or Malacca was possible, if Enrique survived and was given his freedom. Enrique's first-hand knowledge of the Europeans would have made him valuable to merchants and Cebu's raja—giving him something to barter with ... or possibly making too valuable as a slave to release.

Enrique's Origin

It is also possible Enrique had in fact already reached his home islands. According to Magellan the "captured slave" was from Malacca, and Antonio Pigafetta, Magellan's chronicler, said Enrique was from Sumatra. Both could have been correct, since a large area of Sumatra across the strait was Malaccan territory.

But some scholars argue that since Enrique spoke the language at Limasawa, he could have grown up in the region—the Visayan Islands—and was brought to Malacca perhaps already a slave. Malacca did in fact import slaves from as far as the Visayas.

Most likely, though, Enrique was speaking Malay at Limasawa— the language long used in Southeast Asian trade. Antonio Pigafetta's explanation points to that. In a meeting with the raja there, Enrique was able to converse with a Siamese merchant.

> When the king [raja] came near the flagship, the slave spoke to him. The king understood him, for in those districts the kings know more languages than the other people.
>
> The king told him … it was their custom for all ships that entered their ports to pay tribute, and that it was but four days since a junk from Ciama [Siam] laden with gold and slaves had paid him tribute. As proof of his statement the king pointed out to the interpreter a merchant from Ciama, who had remained to trade the gold and slaves. …
>
> Thereupon, the Moro merchant said to the king …"Look well, sire. These men are the same who have conquered Calicut, Malaca, and all India Magiore [Major]. If they are treated well, they will give good treatment, but if they are treated evil, evil and worse treatment, as they have done to Calicut and Malaca."
>
> The interpreter understood it all and told the king that his master's king was more powerful in men and ships than the king of Portogalo, that he was the king of Spagnia and emperor of all the Christians, and that if the king did not care to be his friend he would next time send so many men that they would destroy him.

As for Enrique himself, the feat of circling the earth would have had a very different meaning. For Enrique, reaching Asia, hearing an Austronesian language he knew, meant he had returned or at least nearly returned to his home. As a backdrop he had three years earlier faced the possibility of spending the rest of his life in Portugal or Spain as a slave.

To Enrique circumnavigation wasn't about finding new lands but about returning to familiar ones.

Today, half a millennium later, debate over Magellan's legacy is heated. To many in the West and in Asia, Magellan is a hero, the driving force behind the first circumnavigation. He is one of the great explorers, a national myth taught to schoolchildren in many countries.

To many others, though, Magellan's journey serves as an early and ugly landmark of colonization and the imperialism that came to dominate much of the world until the mid-twentieth century, and indeed still does in places, it is argued, in practice if not in name.

So as people debate the meaning of the voyage—and who gets credit (Magellan, who was killed in the Philippines, or Juan Sebastián Elcano, or all surviving crew?)—it is fitting that the first circumnavigator turned out to be an unlikely hero, neither Spanish nor Portuguese, but rather a young Austronesian slave captured in Malacca a decade earlier.

This was a young man who witnessed first-hand the early forays of colonizing by both the Portuguese (in Malacca) and the Spanish (in South America and the Philippines) half a millennium ago. And traveled from one to the other the long way.

As we question the legacy of Magellan, Columbus, and other explorers, we should stop to appreciate the journey of Enrique of Malacca, whose epic feat was accomplished not through war or greed but through the unlikely paths that fate dealt him.

------

1. A romanticized portrait of Enrique. Magellan's carracks didn't have wheels for steering.

2. Henry the Navigator gained his interest in navigation from his mother, Philippa of Lancaster, who was Queen of Portugal from 1387 until 1415 by marriage to King John I. Philippa gained her interest in geography from one of her tutors back in England, Geoffrey Chaucer.

Photos Credits

Page / Source

15. Pigafetta. Original author unknown. Wikimedia Commons.

16. Pigafetta manuscript spread. Library of Congress.

19. Pigafetta manuscript spread. Library of Congress.

21. Pigafetta 's map of the strait. Library of Congress.

23. Charles V. By Jakob Seisenegger - Kunsthistorisches Museum Wien, Bilddatenbank., Public Domain, Wiki Commons.

26. Charles V map. Barjimoa, CC BY-SA 4.0 Wikimedia Commons.

27. Charles and Isabella. Peter Paul Rubens, Public domain, Wikimedia Commons.

28. Ptolemy map. Lord Nicolas the German (Donnus Nicholas Germanus), cartographerJohann the Blockcutter of Armsheim (Johannes Schnitzer or Johannes de Armssheim), engraver PtolemyJacobus Angelus, translator, Public domain, via Wikimedia Commons.

30. Fra Mauro map. Piero Falchetta, Public domain, via Wikimedia Commons.

32. Martin Waldseemüller's world map. Martin Waldseemüller, Public domain, via Wikimedia Commons.

34. Anonymous Portuguese (1502), smuggled by Cantino. Public domain, via Wikimedia Commons.

36. Diego Ribero, Public domain, via Wikimedia Commons.

38. Magellan-Elcano circumnavigation map. By Magellan_Elcano_Circumnavigation-fr.svg: Sémhurderivative work: Uxbona (talk) - Magellan_Elcano_Circumnavigation-fr.svg, CC BY-SA 3.0.

41. Juan de Cartagena. By L. Bennett - Les premiers explorateurs par Jules Verne, Public Domain, Wikimedia Commons.

45. Dancing Patagonian. Butterworth, Hezekiah. The Story of Magellan and the Discovery of the Philippines. Gutenberg.org.

46. Tehuelches in Argentina. Jessie Tarbox Beals, Public domain, via Wikimedia Commons.

54. Oscar Pereira da Silva (1904). Public domain, Wikimedia Commons.

56. Victoria replica. Gnsin, CC BY-SA 3.0, via Wikimedia Commons.

59. Magellan in strait. Public domain, via Wikimedia Commons.

62. Brunei. Butterworth, Hezekiah. The Story of Magellan and the Discovery of the Philippines. Gutenberg.org.

66. Portuguese trade routes. Walrasiad, CC BY 3.0, via Wikimedia Commons

67. Portuguese trade empire. Creative Commons license. Wikimedia Commons.

73. Magellan. Miscellaneous Items in High Demand, PPOC, Library of Congress, Public domain, via Wikimedia Commons.

74. Serrão. Public domain, Library of Congress.

76. Azamor. Georg Braun; Frans Hogenberg, Public domain, via Wikimedia Commons.

79. Mutiny struggle. Butterworth, Hezekiah. The Story of Magellan and the Discovery of the Philippines. Gutenberg.org.

82. Mactan. Butterworth, Hezekiah. The Story of Magellan and the Discovery of the Philippines. Gutenberg.org.

87. Elcano. Original:Imprenta de Luis TassoPhoto:Fondo Antiguo de la Biblioteca de la Universidad de Sevilla from Sevilla, España, Public domain, via Wikimedia Commons.

89. Around the World in Eighty Days. AnonymousUnknown author, Public domain, via Wikimedia Commons.

93. By Sir John Mandeville. By John Mandeville (created 1459). Via NYPL Digital Gallery, Public Domain.

94. Odoric of Pordenone. By Unknown author; Romance and Travels, 14th century. Reproduction in Genghis Khan et l'Empire Mongol by Jean-Paul Roux, collection "Découvertes Gallimard" (n° 422), série Histoire., Public Domain, Wikimedia Commons.

95. Srivijaya map. Gunawan Kartapranata, CC BY-SA 4.0, via Wikimedia Commons.

96. Borobudur ships. Haddon, A.C., Public domain, via Wikimedia Commons.

98. Enrique of Malaccca. Øyvind Holmstad, CC BY-SA 4.0, via Wikimedia Commons.

99. Malacca. By Gaspar Correia. Internetarchive.org.

About the Author

John Sailors has worked as a writer and editor in the United States and Asia, in educational publishing and as a journalist. He has spent recent years researching the history of maritime trade around the Indian Ocean and Southeast Asia, the Magellan-Elcano expedition, and the beginnings of colonization.

John lives in the San Francisco area. When not doing mindless copyediting (meditating), he can be found reading dictionaries, blowing up video game enemy tanks, and trying to figure out sixteenth-century carracks.

www.ingramcontent.com/pod-product-compliance
Lightning Source LLC
Chambersburg PA
CBHW072042040426
42447CB00012BB/2981